HOW TO BU] MYSTERY BOXES

MW00887005

A STEP BY STEP GUIDE TO DISCOVERING HIDDEN TREASURES

REMY STONE

COPYRIGHT © 2024 BY [REMY STONE]. ALL RIGHTS RESERVED.

NO PART OF THIS BOOK MAY BE COPIED, DISTRIBUTED, OR STORED IN ANY FORM OR THROUGH ANY MEANS, WHETHER ELECTRONIC OR MECHANICAL, WITHOUT THE PRIOR WRITTEN CONSENT OF THE PUBLISHER. EXCEPTIONS INCLUDE BRIEF QUOTATIONS USED IN REVIEWS AND OTHER NON-COMMERCIAL USES AS ALLOWED BY COPYRIGHT LAW.

FIRST EDITION PUBLISHED 2024

BY [REMY STONE]

THIS BOOK HAS BEEN METICULOUSLY PREPARED. THE AUTHOR IS NOT LIABLE FOR ANY ERRORS, OMISSIONS, OR CHANGES TO THE INFORMATION CONTAINED HEREIN. NEITHER THE PUBLISHER NOR THE AUTHOR SHALL BE HELD RESPONSIBLE FOR ANY DAMAGE RESULTING DIRECTLY OR INDIRECTLY FROM THE USE OF THIS MATERIAL.

TABLE OF CONTENTS

DISCLAIMER

THE INFORMATION IN THIS BOOK IS PROVIDED FOR
GENERAL KNOWLEDGE. THE AUTHOR IS NOT
RESPONSIBLE FOR ANY ERRORS OR OMISSIONS, NOR FOR
ANY DAMAGES RESULTING FROM THE USE OF THIS
INFORMATION

INTRODUCTION

The thrill of the unknown and the anticipation of uncovering hidden gems are what make mystery boxes so captivating. Each box holds the promise of something unique, whether it's a rare collectible, a valuable gadget, or an unexpected surprise that brings joy. This guide has aimed to equip you with the tools and insights needed to navigate this intriguing market with confidence.

The strategies and tips shared throughout the book are designed to enhance your experience, ensuring you make informed decisions while indulging in the excitement of mystery boxes. From setting budgets and managing expectations to recognizing reputable sellers and understanding return policies, these elements are crucial in maximizing your satisfaction and minimizing potential risks.

As you venture forth into this fascinating hobby, remember that the true value of a mystery box lies not just in its contents, but in the excitement and curiosity it ignites. Each purchase is an opportunity to explore, to learn, and to enjoy the thrill of discovery. Whether you're a seasoned collector or a curious newcomer, the world of Amazon mystery boxes offers endless possibilities. May the knowledge and insights gained from this guide serve you well as you continue to uncover the hidden treasures that await within each mystery box.

From understanding the intricacies of online marketplaces to mastering the art of evaluating sellers, the knowledge gained is invaluable for those eager to dive into the realm of mystery boxes.

CHAPTER 1

THE ALLURE OF MYSTERY BOXES

Imagine the thrill of unwrapping a package shrouded in mystery, where the contents are as unpredictable as they are intriguing. Such is the allure of Amazon mystery boxes, a modern-day treasure hunt that captivates the imagination of shoppers worldwide. These enigmatic parcels, often filled with a variety of items ranging from the mundane to the extraordinary, offer a unique shopping experience that combines the excitement of a surprise with the potential for discovering unexpected treasures.

The concept of the mystery box taps into a fundamental human curiosity—the desire to explore the unknown. Each box is a sealed promise of adventure, holding within it the possibility of delight, surprise, and even serendipity. As one contemplates the possibilities, the mind races with questions: What could be inside? Will it be something useful, something delightful, or perhaps something entirely unexpected? This element of suspense is what makes the mystery box so alluring and addictive.

Amazon, a giant in the e-commerce world, has embraced this concept, offering mystery boxes that cater to a wide range of interests and budgets. From electronics to fashion, from toys to household gadgets, these boxes can contain a plethora of items, each carefully selected to ensure a varied and intriguing experience for the recipient. The diversity of potential contents means that each box is a unique adventure, a snapshot of the vast array of products available in the digital marketplace.

The popularity of mystery boxes can be attributed to more than just curiosity. There is an undeniable thrill in the act of discovery, in peeling back the layers of packaging to reveal what lies beneath. For many, purchasing a mystery box is a form of entertainment, a way to indulge in the joy of surprise. It's an experience that transcends the ordinary transaction, transforming a simple purchase into an event.

Moreover, the mystery box phenomenon taps into the consumer's desire for value. The appeal of potentially receiving items that far exceed the cost of the box itself adds a layer of excitement. It's a gamble, yes, but one that is tempered by the prospect of unexpected gain. This potential for high reward is part of what makes mystery boxes so enticing.

For those new to the world of Amazon mystery boxes, the journey begins with selecting the right box. With countless options available, each promising a different kind of adventure, the choice can be daunting. However, the process of selection is part of the experience, an opportunity to tailor the adventure to one's personal tastes and interests. Whether seeking the thrill of the unknown or the chance to discover hidden gems, the mystery box offers an unparalleled shopping experience.

In this realm of surprise and anticipation, the mystery box stands as a testament to the enduring appeal of the unknown. It invites us to step away from the predictable and embrace the unexpected, to find joy in the simple act of unboxing, and to relish the moment when the mystery is finally revealed. In a world where much is known and predictable, the mystery box offers a refreshing reminder of the wonder that lies in the unknown.

The History Behind the Hype

Long before the digital age, the allure of mystery and the excitement of the unknown have captivated human curiosity. The concept of the mystery box is not a new phenomenon; it draws its roots from age-old practices that have thrilled and intrigued people for centuries. The idea of purchasing something without knowing its exact contents taps into a primal sense of adventure, the same thrill that ancient treasure hunts and secret auctions once provided.

In the early 20th century, the notion of surprise packages began to gain popularity. These were times when mailorder catalogs were burgeoning, and companies saw an opportunity to clear out unsold inventory by bundling them into 'mystery packages.' Customers, driven by the prospect of receiving something valuable at a fraction of the cost, eagerly participated. This era marked the beginning of a commercial strategy that would evolve significantly over the decades.

The transition from physical to digital platforms brought about a renaissance in the mystery box concept. With the advent of e-commerce giants like Amazon, the potential for mystery boxes expanded exponentially. Amazon, with its vast array of products and global reach, became the perfect stage for this modern-day treasure hunt. Sellers on the platform began to curate these boxes, filled with a mix of overstock, returns, and random items, often with a promise of high-value surprises.

The hype around Amazon mystery boxes is fueled by several factors. The psychology of anticipation plays a significant role; the excitement of not knowing what one might receive is akin to the thrill of gambling. Additionally, the social media era has amplified this phenomenon. Unboxing videos, where influencers and everyday consumers reveal the contents of their mystery boxes, have become viral sensations. These videos not only showcase the element of surprise but also build a community of enthusiasts who share their experiences and discoveries.

Moreover, the economic aspect cannot be overlooked. In a time where consumer behavior is heavily influenced by the prospect of deals and savings, the idea of acquiring potentially high-value items at a low cost is particularly appealing. This economic allure is often accompanied by a sense of exclusivity, as some boxes are marketed as limited editions or themed collections, adding another layer to their desirability.

However, the popularity of these mystery boxes also raises questions about consumer protection and the ethical implications of such sales. While many buyers are thrilled with their purchases, others express disappointment when the contents do not meet their expectations. This dual nature of satisfaction and dissatisfaction keeps the mystery box market dynamic and, at times, contentious.

As the trend continues to evolve, it reflects broader shifts in consumer behavior and the ways in which companies engage with their audiences. The history behind the hype of Amazon mystery boxes is a testament to the enduring appeal of mystery and surprise, a narrative that continues to unfold as both buyers and sellers navigate this intriguing marketplace.

Why People Love Surprises

There's an undeniable allure that accompanies the unknown, a magnetic pull that draws people toward the thrill of uncertainty. This fascination with surprises taps into a deep-seated human desire for novelty and excitement, offering a break from the mundane routines of everyday life. The concept of a mystery box, especially one from a global giant like Amazon, encapsulates this very essence of surprise, promising a blend of anticipation, curiosity, and the potential for unexpected delight.

At its core, the love for surprises is rooted in the element of discovery. Humans are naturally curious creatures, driven by an innate need to explore and uncover hidden treasures. The mystery box serves as a modern-day treasure chest, filled with the promise of discovery waiting to be unveiled. Each box is a sealed enigma, holding within it the potential for joy, intrigue, or even the occasional disappointment, but it is this unpredictability that keeps the experience exhilarating.

The psychological response to surprises is also worth noting. When people encounter the unexpected, their brains release dopamine, a neurotransmitter associated with pleasure and reward. This chemical reaction not only enhances the immediate experience but also builds a positive association with the act of receiving surprises. Over time, this creates a loop of anticipation and fulfillment, making the prospect of opening a mystery box all the more appealing.

Furthermore, surprises offer a form of escapism. In a world where predictability often reigns, the chance to experience something unforeseen can be a welcome reprieve. It allows individuals to momentarily step outside of their structured lives and indulge in a whimsical adventure. The act of opening a mystery box becomes a small but significant event, a moment of suspense and wonder that breaks the monotony and injects a dose of excitement into the day.

There's also a communal aspect to the love for surprises.
The popularity of unboxing videos on platforms like YouTube and social media highlights how people enjoy sharing these experiences with others. Watching someone unveil the contents of a mystery box

can be as thrilling as opening one yourself, creating a shared sense of wonder and anticipation. It fosters a community of enthusiasts who revel in the joys and surprises that each box brings.

Moreover, surprises can evoke nostalgia, harking back to the innocent thrill of childhood when every gift held the promise of magic and mystery. This connection to simpler times can be comforting, providing a sense of joy and wonder that many seek to recapture in adulthood. The mystery box becomes more than just a collection of items; it transforms into a vessel of memories, adventure, and the timeless appeal of the unknown.

In essence, the love for surprises is a complex interplay of curiosity, psychological reward, escapism, communal joy, and nostalgia. It is this multifaceted allure that makes mystery boxes from Amazon such a compelling phenomenon, inviting people to indulge their sense of wonder and explore the delightful unpredictability that each box promises. As long as there is a desire for discovery and the thrill of the unknown, the charm of surprises will continue to captivate and enchant.

The Psychological Appeal

Venturing into the world of Amazon mystery boxes is much like stepping into a realm where the boundaries of anticipation and curiosity blur, creating an intoxicating blend of emotions that captivate the human psyche. At the heart of this allure is the psychological thrill that draws individuals into the mystique of the unknown. This phenomenon is deeply rooted in the fundamental aspects of human nature, tapping into innate desires and emotional responses that have been honed over millennia.

The allure of mystery boxes lies in the unpredictable nature of their contents. This uncertainty triggers a complex emotional cocktail, primarily driven by the element of surprise. The human brain is wired to seek novelty and excitement, and mystery boxes offer just that. They provide an opportunity to experience a rush akin to that of gambling, where the outcome is uncertain, and the potential rewards are tantalizing. The anticipation of opening a mystery box can be as exhilarating as the unboxing itself, creating a sense of suspense that keeps the consumer engaged.

Moreover, there is a psychological concept known as 'intermittent reinforcement,' which plays a significant role in the appeal of mystery boxes. This concept explains how unpredictable rewards can be more enticing than predictable ones. When consumers purchase a mystery box, they are effectively rolling the dice, hoping for that rare or valuable item. This unpredictability can create a powerful loop of excitement and satisfaction, as each purchase holds the promise of uncovering a hidden gem.

Another layer to the psychological appeal is the sense of adventure and discovery. Humans have an inherent desire for exploration and uncovering new experiences. Mystery boxes tap into this instinct, offering a mini-adventure with each unboxing. The act of revealing unknown contents can evoke a sense of nostalgia, reminiscent of childhood experiences of opening gifts.

Social factors also contribute significantly to the psychological draw of mystery boxes. In an age where social media plays a pivotal role in shaping consumer behavior, the unboxing experience is often shared online, creating a community of enthusiasts who revel in the shared experience of discovery. This social interaction can amplify the excitement, as individuals seek to share their finds and connect with others who share their interests.

Additionally, the perceived value of the mystery box often outweighs the actual value of its contents. This perception is influenced by the marketing techniques used to promote these boxes, which often highlight the potential for highvalue items. The disparity between perceived and actual value can enhance the sense of satisfaction when the contents are revealed, even if they do not meet objective expectations.

In essence, the psychological appeal of Amazon mystery boxes is a multifaceted phenomenon that taps into deepseated human emotions and desires. It combines the thrill of the unknown with the joy of discovery, all while leveraging social dynamics to create an engaging and addictive experience. This intricate interplay of factors ensures that the allure of mystery boxes continues to captivate consumers, drawing them into a world where the next great find could be just a box away.

CHAPTER 2

EXPLORING AMAZON MARKETPLACE

Getting Started on Amazon

Navigating the vast realm of Amazon can initially appear daunting, especially for those eager to delve into the intriguing world of mystery boxes. As you prepare to explore this unique shopping experience, it is essential to familiarize yourself with the basic steps and features of the Amazon platform. This foundational knowledge will ensure a seamless and enjoyable journey as you hunt for those elusive packages filled with surprises.

The first step in this adventure is to establish an Amazon account. Visit the Amazon website and locate the 'Create Account' option, typically found at the top right corner of the homepage. The process of setting up an account is straightforward, requiring basic information such as your name, email address, and a secure password. Once your account is created, take a moment to explore your account settings. Here, you can add and manage your delivery addresses, set up payment methods, and adjust your preferences to tailor the Amazon experience to your needs.

With your account ready, the next phase is to familiarize yourself with Amazon's search functionality. The search bar, prominently displayed at the top of every page, is your gateway to discovering the myriad products available on Amazon. For those specifically interested in mystery boxes, typing keywords like 'mystery box' or 'surprise box' into the search bar will yield a variety of options across different categories and themes. As you scroll through the results, you will notice various filters on the left-hand side of the page. These filters allow you to narrow down your search based on price range, customer reviews, and sellers, among other criteria, enhancing your ability to find the perfect mystery box.

Understanding the product pages is crucial in your exploration. Each product listing provides detailed information, including product descriptions, seller details, and customer reviews. Pay close attention to the product description to understand what type of items might be included in the mystery box and any specific themes it might follow. Customer reviews and ratings are invaluable resources, offering insights from previous buyers about the quality and satisfaction of the product. These reviews can guide your decision-making process, helping you avoid potential disappointments.

It is also important to become acquainted with Amazon's Prime membership benefits, which can significantly enhance your purchasing experience. Prime members enjoy advantages such as expedited shipping, exclusive deals, and early access to new products. If you are planning frequent purchases or want to ensure quick delivery of your mystery boxes, considering a Prime membership might be worthwhile.

Lastly, understanding Amazon's return policies is vital, especially when dealing with mystery boxes where the contents are unknown. Familiarize yourself with the return process and any associated terms to ensure a smooth transaction in case the delivered items do not meet your expectations. By grasping these foundational elements of Amazon's platform, you are well-prepared to dive into the thrilling pursuit of mystery boxes, ready to uncover the surprises that await inside each package.

Understanding Amazon's Ecosystem

Navigating the vast and intricate world of Amazon is akin to exploring a bustling metropolis, each corner offering a different experience and opportunity. To truly grasp the potential of Amazon mystery boxes, one must first understand the complex ecosystem that Amazon has meticulously crafted over the years. This ecosystem is not just a marketplace; it is a dynamic environment where sellers, buyers, and algorithms interact in a seamless dance of commerce.

At the heart of Amazon's ecosystem is its highly sophisticated algorithm, often referred to as A9. This algorithm is responsible for determining which products appear in search results, thus influencing what buyers see and ultimately purchase. The importance of keywords, product descriptions, and customer reviews cannot be overstated, as these elements are critical in ensuring a product's visibility in such a competitive marketplace. For those interested in

Amazon mystery boxes, understanding how these factors play into the algorithm can be the difference between discovering a hidden gem and sifting through unwanted items.

Amazon's Prime membership is another pivotal component of its ecosystem. With over 200 million members worldwide, Prime offers benefits such as free shipping, exclusive deals, and access to streaming services. This membership not only enhances the shopping experience but also encourages frequent purchases, creating a cycle of consumption that benefits sellers and buyers alike. For mystery box enthusiasts, being a Prime member can provide access to exclusive deals and faster shipping, making the hunt for the perfect box even more enticing.

The Fulfilled by Amazon (FBA) program is a cornerstone of the ecosystem, providing sellers with the infrastructure needed to reach millions of customers. Through FBA, Amazon handles storage, packaging, and shipping, allowing sellers to focus on sourcing and marketing their products. For those purchasing mystery boxes, this means a consistent delivery experience and often quicker shipping times. Additionally, the reliability associated with FBA can give buyers confidence in their purchases, knowing that Amazon's stringent standards are applied to the sellers who use this service.

Customer reviews and ratings are the lifeblood of Amazon's ecosystem, influencing purchasing decisions and seller reputations. For mystery box buyers, reviews can provide insights into the contents and quality of the boxes, helping them make informed choices. Sellers, on the other hand, rely on positive reviews to build trust and credibility, making it imperative for them to maintain high standards of quality and customer service.

Amazon's ecosystem is also characterized by its global reach and diverse product offerings. With marketplaces in numerous countries, Amazon provides an unparalleled selection of products, including mystery boxes from various regions. This diversity not only enriches the shopping experience but also allows buyers to access unique items that may not be available locally.

Understanding Amazon's ecosystem is essential for anyone looking to delve into the world of mystery boxes. By recognizing the interplay of algorithms, membership benefits, fulfillment services, and customer feedback, buyers can navigate this complex environment with confidence, maximizing their chances of uncovering exciting and valuable surprises within their mystery boxes.

Navigating the Marketplace

Stepping into the expansive world of Amazon's marketplace feels akin to entering a bustling bazaar filled with endless possibilities and hidden treasures. The allure of mystery boxes, with their promise of surprise and potential value, draws many into this vibrant ecosystem. Yet, as with any vast market, navigating it requires a keen eye, strategic approach, and a touch of patience.

Firstly, understanding the layout of the Amazon marketplace is crucial. The platform is a complex network of listings, each vying for attention. Mystery boxes are often listed under various categories, sometimes tucked away in the 'Deals' section or featured prominently in flash sales. A thorough exploration of these areas can yield intriguing prospects, each box offering a unique blend of items that could range from everyday essentials to rare collectibles.

One of the primary considerations when navigating this marketplace is the seller's reputation. Amazon's vastness means that sellers vary greatly in reliability and quality. It's essential to scrutinize seller ratings and reviews meticulously. A seller with consistent positive feedback is more likely to provide a mystery box that aligns with expectations, ensuring that the contents are worth the investment. Conversely, a seller with mixed or negative reviews might be a gamble that could lead to disappointment.

Another aspect to consider is the description of the mystery box itself. While the contents are, by nature, a surprise, reputable sellers usually provide a general outline of what one might expect. This could include categories of items, potential brands, or the type of products included. Carefully reading these descriptions helps in setting realistic expectations and avoiding any potential dissatisfaction. Additionally, it's wise to compare similar offerings from different sellers to gauge the best value proposition.

Price is often a significant factor in decision-making. The allure of a low-priced mystery box can be tempting, but it's important to weigh this against the potential quality and quantity of items. Sometimes, investing a little more in a box from a well-reviewed seller can yield better results than opting for a cheaper alternative with uncertain contents. It's about balancing cost with the potential for discovery and satisfaction.

Navigating the marketplace also involves timing. Amazon frequently updates its listings, and mystery boxes can appear and disappear quickly. Setting alerts or frequently checking the marketplace can increase the chances of snagging a coveted box. Additionally, participating in Amazon's periodic sales events can offer opportunities to purchase these boxes at discounted rates, enhancing the value of the exploration.

Lastly, engaging with the community can provide invaluable insights. Online forums and review sites often have discussions about the latest offerings, with members sharing their experiences and recommendations. This collective wisdom can guide new buyers towards reputable sellers and highlight which mystery boxes have delivered delightful surprises.

In this intricate dance of exploration and anticipation, the marketplace becomes not just a place to purchase, but a realm of discovery. With careful navigation, the pursuit of Amazon mystery boxes transforms into an exciting expedition, where each selection promises the thrill of the unknown and the joy of uncovering hidden gems.

In the vast expanse of Amazon's marketplace, mystery boxes hold a particular allure, akin to treasure chests waiting to be unearthed. The thrill of discovery is at the heart of this pursuit, where each box promises the unknown, a potential trove of hidden gems that could range from the mundane to the extraordinary. As you navigate this intriguing world, the key lies in honing the art of discernment, a skill that can transform the experience from a mere gamble to a calculated exploration.

The journey begins with understanding the subtle cues that hint at the quality of a mystery box. Sellers often provide vague descriptions, but within these words lie clues that can guide your decision. Pay attention to the language used; terms like "surplus," "overstock," and "liquidation" can indicate the type of items you might find inside. A deeper dive into seller reviews and ratings can reveal patterns of satisfaction or disappointment among previous buyers, offering valuable insights into the likelihood of uncovering treasures.

Photographs, though sparse and sometimes absent, are another tool at your disposal. When available, scrutinize them for any hints about the box's contents. Look for recognizable brand names or packaging that suggests highvalue items. While the mystery is part of the allure, a keen eye can often spot subtle indicators that make one box more appealing than another.

Timing also plays a crucial role in the quest for hidden gems. Certain times of the year, such as post-holiday seasons, can be particularly fruitful as retailers clear out excess inventory. During these periods, mystery boxes may contain unsold items that didn't meet the holiday rush but still hold significant value.

Moreover, consider the seller's reputation in the wider context of the marketplace. Established sellers with a history of positive feedback are more likely to offer boxes that contain worthwhile items. Engage with the community of mystery box enthusiasts through forums and social media groups. These platforms are rich with shared experiences and tips, offering a collective wisdom that can guide you towards the most promising finds.

The thrill of seeking out hidden gems in Amazon mystery boxes is not just about the physical contents you acquire but also about the stories these items tell. Each discovery is a narrative, a snapshot of consumer trends, and sometimes, a glimpse into the unexpected creativity of product design. As you delve deeper into this world, you develop an intuitive sense of what makes a mystery box worth the plunge.

Ultimately, the pursuit of hidden gems within Amazon mystery boxes is an exercise in curiosity and patience. It invites you to embrace the unknown with a strategic mind, balancing the excitement of chance with informed decisionmaking. With each box opened, you refine your ability to discern value amidst uncertainty, transforming the act of buying into a rewarding adventure of exploration and discovery.

CHAPTER 3

TYPES OF MYSTERY BOXES AVALIABLE

Tech and Gadgets

In the ever-evolving landscape of online shopping, Amazon mystery boxes have emerged as a tantalizing enigma, especially for tech enthusiasts and gadget aficionados. These intriguing packages, shrouded in secrecy, promise a thrill akin to unwrapping a surprise gift on a festive morning. Each box holds the potential to unveil a treasure trove of gadgets, ranging from the latest smart devices to quirky tech accessories. As you delve into the world of Amazon mystery boxes, you'll find that it's a realm where curiosity meets technology, and the allure of the unknown beckons.

Within this digital marketplace, the concept of mystery boxes taps into the innate human desire for surprise and discovery. The tech and gadgets category stands out as one of the most popular, fueled by the rapid pace of technological advancements and the constant craving for the next big thing. Opening a mystery box can feel like gaining access to a secret vault of innovation, where each item is a piece of the puzzle that defines modern living.

Imagine the thrill of tearing into a box to find a sleek new smartwatch, its face gleaming with the promise of connectivity and convenience. Or perhaps you unveil a pair of wireless earbuds, the kind that seamlessly sync with your devices, offering a soundtrack to your daily adventures. The anticipation of what lies within is part of the magic, driving many to invest in these enigmatic parcels time and again.

Yet, the experience is not solely about the products themselves; it's about the stories they tell and the possibilities they unlock. A virtual reality headset might transport you to distant worlds, allowing you to explore landscapes beyond your wildest dreams. A portable charger, though seemingly mundane, becomes a lifeline in your tech arsenal, ensuring your gadgets remain powered during those crucial moments.

The diversity of items that can be found in tech and gadget mystery boxes is astounding. From cutting-edge smart home devices that transform your living space into a futuristic haven to quirky tech toys that provide endless amusement, each box is a testament to the boundless creativity of the tech industry. The joy of discovery is complemented by the satisfaction of acquiring gadgets that integrate seamlessly into your lifestyle, enhancing productivity, entertainment, and connectivity.

However, navigating the world of Amazon mystery boxes requires a discerning eye and a sense of adventure. Reviews and ratings from fellow buyers can offer valuable insights, helping you gauge the potential value and quality of the contents. While some boxes may exceed expectations, others might present an eclectic mix of items that challenge your imagination. The element of risk is part of the allure, a gamble that can result in unexpected delight or a lesson in managing expectations.

Ultimately, the tech and gadgets mystery box phenomenon is a testament to the enduring appeal of surprise in a world where predictability often reigns. It's a celebration of technology's endless possibilities and a reminder that, sometimes, the most rewarding experiences come from embracing the unknown. Whether you're a seasoned tech enthusiast or a curious newcomer, the promise of what lies within these boxes continues to captivate and inspire.

Fashion and Accessories

Imagine peeling back the layers of a neatly sealed Amazon mystery box, each layer revealing a tantalizing glimpse into a world of fashion where anticipation mingles with surprise. The allure of these boxes lies not only in their concealed contents but also in the promise of discovering hidden gems that could redefine your style. As the cardboard flaps are lifted, the excitement is palpable, akin to opening a treasure chest brimming with sartorial possibilities. Within these boxes, the world of fashion unfolds in myriad forms, from avant-garde accessories to timeless wardrobe staples, each piece a potential cornerstone of your personal style narrative.

The journey begins with the rustle of tissue paper, unveiling a cascade of colors, textures, and patterns that beckon exploration. You might find a silk scarf with an intricate paisley design, its soft sheen catching the light and inviting your touch. Draping it across your shoulders, you can almost feel the elegance it lends to even the simplest outfit. Next, perhaps, a pair of sunglasses emerges, their sleek frames and tinted lenses offering a chic shield against the sun's glare, while simultaneously elevating your fashion quotient.

A mystery box could also hold a statement necklace, its bold beads and metallic accents offering a striking contrast against a plain blouse. The weight of it around your neck is both comforting and empowering, a tangible reminder of the transformative power of accessories. As you delve deeper, a belt might appear, its leather supple and its buckle adorned with intricate engravings. Cinching it around your waist, you notice how it effortlessly defines your silhouette, adding a touch of sophistication to your ensemble.

Among the treasures, you may discover a handbag, its design a perfect blend of function and fashion. The craftsmanship is evident in the stitching, the quality of the material, and the thoughtful layout of its compartments, all of which speak to its potential as a reliable companion for daily adventures. As you explore further, a pair of earrings might catch your eye, their delicate design and subtle sparkle capturing light with every movement. These small yet significant pieces have the power to frame your face beautifully, adding a hint of glamour to your overall look.

A mystery box's magic lies not only in the tangible items it contains but also in the inspiration it sparks. Each piece holds the potential to reinvigorate your wardrobe, encouraging you to experiment with new styles and combinations you might not have considered before. The thrill of the unknown, coupled with the joy of discovery, makes each unboxing an exhilarating experience, one that invites you to step outside your fashion comfort zone.

As you sift through the contents, you realize that these boxes offer more than just accessories; they provide a canvas for self-expression, a means to articulate your unique style in ways both subtle and bold. With each item, you uncover, you're not merely adding to your collection but enhancing your fashion narrative, piece by piece, layer by layer. In the world of Amazon mystery boxes, fashion and accessories become a playground of endless possibilities, where the only limit is your imagination.

Home and Lifestyle

In the world of Amazon mystery boxes, the concept of home and lifestyle is a treasure trove waiting to be uncovered. These boxes often contain a variety of items designed to enhance the comfort and functionality of your living space. Imagine opening a box to find a set of plush, high-quality towels that elevate the ambiance of your bathroom, or perhaps a sleek, modern lamp that adds a touch of elegance to your living room. The allure of these mystery boxes lies in their ability to surprise and delight with each unboxing, offering a curated selection of products that cater to your personal aesthetic and practical needs.

One of the key elements that make home and lifestyle mystery boxes so appealing is the diversity of items they can contain. From decorative pieces like vases and wall art to practical gadgets such as smart home devices and kitchen tools, these boxes are a gateway to discovering new products that you might not have considered purchasing individually. The thrill of not knowing what you will receive adds an element of excitement to the process, transforming the mundane task of shopping into an adventure filled with potential discoveries.

For those who value sustainability and eco-friendliness, some mystery boxes focus on providing environmentally conscious products. You might uncover bamboo utensils, organic cotton linens, or energy-efficient appliances, all of which contribute to a greener lifestyle. This aspect of mystery boxes not only enhances your home but also aligns with a growing awareness of the importance of sustainable living.

Moreover, these boxes can be tailored to fit various tastes and preferences, making them an ideal choice for anyone looking to refresh their home decor or try out new lifestyle products. Whether you prefer a minimalist aesthetic or a more eclectic style, there's a mystery box out there that aligns with your vision. This customization allows you to explore different themes and styles without the commitment of purchasing each item individually, offering a cost-effective way to experiment with your home environment.

The convenience of having a box delivered directly to your doorstep cannot be overstated. In our fast-paced world, the time saved from not having to browse endless product listings is a significant advantage. Instead, you can focus on the joy of receiving a thoughtfully curated selection of items, each with the potential to enhance your living space or daily routine.

Furthermore, these mystery boxes can serve as a source of inspiration for home improvement projects or lifestyle changes. Discovering a new kitchen gadget might inspire you to try cooking a new dish, while a set of yoga accessories could be the push you need to start a new fitness regimen. The serendipitous nature of these boxes encourages exploration and creativity, allowing you to see your home and lifestyle in a new light.

In the realm of Amazon mystery boxes, home and lifestyle offerings provide a unique blend of practicality, surprise, and inspiration. They invite you to reimagine your living space, discover innovative products, and embrace the excitement of the unknown, all while staying true to your personal style and preferences.

Collectibles and Toys

In the realm of Amazon mystery boxes, few categories evoke as much excitement and nostalgia as collectibles and toys. These boxes, often a treasure trove of childhood memories and rare finds, hold a unique allure for both seasoned collectors and casual buyers. The anticipation of uncovering a long-sought-after action figure or a limited edition toy can transform the simple act of opening a box into a thrilling adventure.

When purchasing mystery boxes filled with collectibles and toys, it is crucial to understand the vast array of possibilities that may lie within. These boxes can contain a variety of items ranging from vintage action figures, exclusive Funko Pop! vinyls, die-cast cars, and even trading card sets. The unpredictability of the contents is precisely what makes these boxes so enticing. Each one holds the potential to reveal a hidden gem or a piece that completes a cherished collection.

A key aspect to consider when buying these mystery boxes is the reputation of the seller. Browsing through reviews and ratings can provide valuable insights into the likelihood of receiving quality items. Sellers with a history of satisfied customers and positive feedback are more likely to offer boxes that meet or exceed expectations. Additionally, some sellers may provide a general theme or hint about the contents, such as focusing on a particular franchise like Star Wars or Marvel, which can guide buyers in selecting boxes that align with their interests.

Price is another factor to weigh carefully. While the allure of potentially discovering a rare collectible can be tempting, it's important to set a budget and manage expectations. Mystery boxes range widely in price, often reflecting the perceived value of the potential items inside. Higher-priced boxes might promise a greater chance of containing highvalue or rare items, but this is not always guaranteed.

Balancing the thrill of the unknown with financial prudence ensures that the experience remains enjoyable.

For those new to the world of collectibles and toys, mystery boxes can serve as an exciting introduction. They offer an opportunity to explore various franchises and discover new interests. However, for seasoned collectors, these boxes might represent a gamble, as they might receive duplicate items or pieces that do not fit their specific collections. In such cases, online communities and forums can be invaluable resources for trading or selling unwanted items, allowing collectors to refine their collections while connecting with fellow enthusiasts.

Storage and display considerations should not be overlooked when diving into the world of collectibles. As collections grow, finding appropriate ways to store and showcase these treasures becomes essential. Protective cases, shelves, and display cabinets can help preserve the condition of valuable items while also highlighting their beauty and uniqueness.

Ultimately, the joy of buying Amazon mystery boxes filled with collectibles and toys lies in the element of surprise and the possibility of discovering something truly special.

Whether it's for the thrill of the hunt, the nostalgia of childhood memories, or the excitement of expanding a collection, these boxes offer a unique experience that captivates the imagination and brings a sense of wonder to collectors of all ages.

CHAPTER 4:

ELEVATING SELLERS CREDIBILITY

In the vast digital marketplace that is Amazon, mystery boxes have emerged as a tantalizing gamble for consumers, offering the allure of the unknown and the potential for hidden treasures. However, before diving into the world of mystery boxes, it is essential to navigate the landscape of sellers to ensure a rewarding experience. The first step in this journey is to thoroughly research the sellers offering these enigmatic packages.

The sheer volume of sellers on Amazon can be overwhelming, each promising unique mystery boxes filled with diverse items. To begin, it is crucial to examine the seller's profile meticulously. This includes looking into their ratings and reviews, which provide invaluable insights into the experiences of previous buyers. A seller with consistently high ratings and positive feedback is often a reliable choice, indicating a history of satisfactory transactions. Conversely, a pattern of negative reviews might be a red flag, suggesting potential issues with the quality or delivery of their mystery boxes.

Another important aspect is the seller's tenure on the platform. A seller who has been active for a longer period typically has more experience and a track record that can be evaluated. New sellers might offer enticing deals, but without an established reputation, there is an inherent risk involved. It is wise to balance the allure of a bargain with the assurance of reliability.

Additionally, the product descriptions provided by sellers can be a treasure trove of information. While the very nature of mystery boxes is to remain a surprise, reputable sellers will often provide hints or themes that can guide your expectations. Look for detailed descriptions that specify categories of items or potential brand inclusions. This transparency not only builds trust but also allows you to make a more informed purchasing decision.

Engaging directly with the seller can also be beneficial. Many sellers are open to answering questions or providing additional details about their mystery boxes. This interaction can offer further assurance of the seller's legitimacy and commitment to customer satisfaction.

Moreover, it presents an opportunity to gauge the responsiveness and professionalism of the seller, which are critical factors in any online transaction.

Price comparison is another crucial element of researching sellers. While mystery boxes are inherently unpredictable, comparing prices among different sellers can help identify any outliers that might suggest either a great deal or a potential scam. It is important to find a balance between cost and value, ensuring that the price aligns with the expected quality and quantity of items.

Lastly, consider the seller's return and refund policies. Even with thorough research, there is always an element of risk in purchasing mystery boxes. A seller with a fair and clear return policy provides an added layer of security, allowing you to make your purchase with greater confidence.

In the world of Amazon mystery boxes, the excitement of the unknown is matched by the necessity for careful research. By taking the time to evaluate sellers based on their reviews, tenure, descriptions, communication, pricing, and policies, you can enhance your chances of uncovering a truly delightful surprise.

Reading Reviews

Perusing the reviews of Amazon mystery boxes is akin to stepping into a bustling marketplace filled with eager voices, each vying to share their tales of discovery and delight, or sometimes, disappointment. As you navigate through the sea of opinions, you begin to notice patterns and themes that emerge from the cacophony of experiences. Some reviewers paint vivid pictures of their unboxing adventures, describing the thrill of peeling back layers of anticipation to reveal an eclectic mix of treasures hidden within. They speak of the adrenaline rush that accompanies the unknown, likening it to a modern-day treasure hunt where the prize is as much about the journey as it is about the contents.

In contrast, other reviews strike a more cautious tone, where the thrill of surprise is tempered with the reality of unmet expectations. These voices offer a sobering reminder that mystery boxes, by their very nature, are a gamble. They recount stories of boxes that contained items of little value or relevance, leaving the recipient with a sense of being shortchanged. Such reviews often serve as cautionary tales, urging potential buyers to weigh the risks and manage their expectations before taking the plunge.

Among the myriad of opinions, there are those who provide detailed analyses of the contents, breaking down the perceived value of each item against the price paid. These reviewers often offer insights into the trends and patterns they have observed across multiple purchases, providing a more analytical perspective on the mystery box phenomenon. They discuss the frequency of certain items, the quality of goods, and the overall satisfaction derived from the purchase, offering a comprehensive overview that can be invaluable for prospective buyers.

The reviews also reveal a diverse community of enthusiasts who find joy in sharing their experiences with fellow mystery box aficionados. For some, the excitement of unboxing is amplified by the opportunity to connect with others who share their passion. They exchange tips on where to find the best deals, speculate on the origins of the items, and celebrate each other's finds, fostering a sense of camaraderie and shared adventure.

As you delve deeper into the reviews, you begin to appreciate the varied motivations that drive individuals to purchase these enigmatic parcels. For some, it is the allure of the unknown and the possibility of discovering something truly unique. For others, it is the thrill of collecting and curating a personal trove of curiosities. And then there are those who simply enjoy the element of surprise, finding joy in the unpredictability of what lies within.

In this vibrant tapestry of opinions, each review offers a glimpse into the personal experiences and perspectives of those who have ventured into the world of Amazon mystery boxes. Whether they sing praises or sound warnings, they collectively enrich the narrative of what it means to embrace the mystery, providing valuable insights for anyone considering embarking on their own unboxing adventure. As you read through these accounts, you are invited to weigh the voices, sift through the stories, and ultimately, make your own informed decision about whether to take the leap into the unknown.

Identifying Red Flags

In the thrilling world of Amazon mystery boxes, the allure of the unknown captivates the imaginations of curious buyers. However, beneath the surface of this intriguing market lies a landscape peppered with potential pitfalls that can ensnare the unwary. Recognizing the red flags is a crucial skill for anyone venturing into this realm, ensuring that the excitement of discovery is not overshadowed by disappointment or loss.

One of the most telling indicators of a potentially problematic mystery box is the lack of detailed information or transparency from the seller. Reputable sellers typically provide at least some level of description regarding the types of items included, such as electronics, clothing, or toys. If a listing is conspicuously vague, offering little more than enticing adjectives without substance, it may be a sign that the contents are not as valuable or exciting as implied.

Equally important is the reputation of the seller. In the digital marketplace, feedback and reviews serve as the modern-day word of mouth. A seller with numerous negative reviews or unresolved complaints should be approached with caution. Pay particular attention to comments about the quality of the items received and the accuracy of the listing. A pattern of dissatisfied customers often points to systemic issues that could affect your own purchasing experience.

The price point of a mystery box can also be a red flag. While bargains are a key attraction, prices that seem too good to be true often are. Extremely low-priced boxes may contain items that are damaged, obsolete, or of negligible value. Conversely, exorbitantly priced boxes with no clear justification for their cost should also raise suspicion. It's essential to strike a balance, seeking value without falling for scams.

Another warning sign is a seller's reluctance to provide a return policy or guarantee. A lack of recourse if the box contents are unsatisfactory can leave buyers with little more than regret. Reputable sellers often offer some form of satisfaction guarantee, allowing buyers to return the product if it does not meet expectations.

Finally, be wary of listings that employ high-pressure tactics, such as limited-time offers or claims of scarcity. These strategies are often used to rush buyers into making decisions without due diligence. Taking the time to research and compare can prevent impulsive purchases that lead to disappointment.

Navigating the world of Amazon mystery boxes requires a keen eye and an analytical mindset. By remaining vigilant for these red flags, buyers can protect themselves from common pitfalls, ensuring that the experience of unboxing holds only pleasant surprises. As with any purchase, informed decision-making is the key to unlocking the true potential of mystery boxes, transforming them into a source of joy and discovery rather than a Pandora's box of unwanted surprises.

Trustworthy Transactions

In the realm of Amazon mystery boxes, the thrill of the unknown is as palpable as the excitement of unboxing a surprise gift. However, amidst the allure and anticipation, ensuring trustworthy transactions becomes paramount to safeguard against the pitfalls of deceit and disappointment. Navigating this digital marketplace requires a keen eye and an understanding of the nuances that define reliable purchases.

The foundation of any trustworthy transaction lies in identifying reputable sellers. On platforms like Amazon, where mystery boxes are sold by various vendors, it is crucial to scrutinize seller ratings and reviews. A high rating, coupled with positive feedback, often indicates a seller's reliability and the quality of their offerings. Delving deeper into the reviews can offer insights into other buyers' experiences, shedding light on the seller's consistency in delivering what they promise.

Transparency is another cornerstone of trustworthy transactions. Reputable sellers provide detailed descriptions of their mystery boxes, outlining the categories of items included, potential value, and any specific themes. While the essence of a mystery box is its unpredictability, an honest seller will ensure that buyers have a clear understanding of what to expect in terms of item variety and potential surprises. This clarity not only builds trust but also enhances the overall buying experience by aligning expectations.

In the digital age, secure payment options are vital. Utilizing trusted payment gateways that offer buyer protection can safeguard your purchase. Services such as Amazon Pay, PayPal, or credit card payments with fraud protection features can provide an added layer of security, ensuring that your financial information remains confidential and that you have recourse in case of a dispute.

Moreover, understanding the return and refund policies is essential. A trustworthy seller will have clear and fair policies in place, which are easily accessible and comprehensible. This transparency allows buyers to feel confident in their purchase, knowing that they have options should the mystery box not meet their expectations or if any issues arise. Reading these policies beforehand can prevent misunderstandings and ensure a smoother transaction process.

Communication is key in establishing trust between buyers and sellers. Engaging with the seller before making a purchase can provide reassurance and clarity. Reliable sellers are often responsive and willing to address any queries or concerns, demonstrating their commitment to customer satisfaction. This interaction not only builds confidence in the transaction but also fosters a relationship that can lead to more positive experiences in the future.

As the popularity of mystery boxes continues to grow, so does the importance of fostering an environment of trust and reliability. By prioritizing reputable sellers, ensuring transparency, utilizing secure payment methods, understanding return policies, and maintaining open communication, buyers can navigate the world of Amazon mystery boxes with confidence. These steps are not merely transactional; they are the building blocks of a trustworthy and enjoyable shopping experience that keeps the spirit of mystery alive, while simultaneously protecting the buyer's interests.

CHAPTER 5:

BUDGETING FOR MYSTERY BOX PURCHASES

In the intriguing world of Amazon mystery boxes, the excitement of the unknown mingles with the thrill of potential discovery. Yet, amidst this exhilarating uncertainty, lies the crucial task of setting a budget. This foundational step serves as your compass, guiding your exploration and ensuring that the allure of these enigmatic parcels does not lead you astray financially.

The first consideration in setting a budget is understanding your personal financial landscape. This involves a candid assessment of your disposable income, accounting for all necessary expenses and commitments. By clearly defining what you can afford to allocate towards mystery boxes, you create a safe boundary that protects your financial health while allowing room for enjoyment.

Once you have a clear picture of your financial situation, it's essential to determine the frequency and scale of your purchases. Are you a casual buyer, indulging in a mystery box occasionally as a special treat? Or do you envision yourself as a more frequent seeker, regularly diving into the unknown? This decision will influence how you distribute your budget over time, ensuring that your spending aligns with your buying habits and personal goals.

As you contemplate your financial commitment, it's also important to weigh the potential risks and rewards. Mystery boxes offer the promise of surprise and value, yet they are inherently unpredictable. This uncertainty is part of their charm, but it also means that the contents may not always meet your expectations or desires. By setting a budget, you acknowledge and accept this variability, allowing you to enjoy the experience without undue stress or disappointment.

A practical approach to budgeting for mystery boxes involves establishing a dedicated fund or account. By setting aside a specific amount of money exclusively for this purpose, you create a tangible boundary that separates your mystery box purchases from other financial obligations. This method not only helps you adhere to your budget but also enhances the sense of anticipation and excitement, as you watch your mystery box fund grow over time.

In addition to financial considerations, setting a budget encourages thoughtful decision-making. It prompts you to research and evaluate different mystery box options, comparing prices, contents, and reviews. This careful consideration can lead to more satisfying purchases, as you become a discerning buyer who selects boxes that align with your interests and expectations.

Ultimately, setting a budget is not just about limiting your spending; it's about enhancing your overall experience. By defining clear financial boundaries, you empower yourself to explore the world of Amazon mystery boxes with confidence and peace of mind. This structured approach allows you to savor the thrill of the unknown, knowing that you are in control of your financial journey. With a wellconsidered budget, you can fully immerse yourself in the adventure, embracing each mystery box as a delightful opportunity to discover something new and unexpected.

Cost vs Value

When considering the purchase of Amazon mystery boxes, a critical factor to evaluate is the relationship between cost and value. This assessment is not merely about calculating the financial expense but also involves understanding the perceived worth of the items contained within these enigma-filled packages. Buyers often find themselves at the crossroads of excitement and skepticism, trying to decipher whether the allure of mystery boxes justifies the price tag attached to them.

The cost of a mystery box is straightforward – it is the monetary amount you pay upfront. However, the value derived from these boxes is multifaceted. It encompasses not only the tangible items received but also the intangible thrill and anticipation associated with unboxing. For some, the sheer joy of discovering unexpected treasures can outweigh the actual monetary value of the items. This emotional satisfaction is a key component that influences purchasing decisions, often tipping the scales in favor of acquiring these boxes.

However, the perceived value is subjective and can vary significantly from one person to another. A box that holds immense value for one individual might be seen as a collection of trivial items by someone else. This disparity often hinges on personal preferences, interests, and expectations. For instance, a mystery box containing tech gadgets might be a goldmine for a tech enthusiast, delivering substantial value beyond the purchase price.

Conversely, the same box might hold little to no value for someone uninterested in such gadgets.

Another layer to consider is the element of risk versus reward. Mystery boxes are, by nature, a gamble. The cost is certain, but the value remains uncertain until the box is opened. This uncertainty can be part of the appeal, offering a sense of adventure and surprise. However, it also introduces the risk of disappointment if the contents do not align with the buyer's expectations or if the perceived value falls short of the cost.

Savvy buyers often mitigate this risk by researching sellers, reading reviews, and setting realistic expectations. Some sellers provide clues or themes about the contents, which can help potential buyers make informed decisions. Additionally, understanding the average retail value of items typically found in these boxes can aid in assessing whether the potential value justifies the cost.

In the realm of Amazon mystery boxes, cost versus value is a dynamic equation influenced by both objective and subjective factors. It requires a careful weighing of financial expense against personal satisfaction and perceived worth. For those who relish the thrill of the unknown, the value may transcend the monetary cost, offering a unique experience that goes beyond the physical items received. On the other hand, buyers focused solely on tangible returns might find the value elusive if the contents do not meet their expectations.

Ultimately, the decision to purchase an Amazon mystery box hinges on individual priorities and the willingness to embrace the unpredictability inherent in these intriguing packages. By understanding the nuances of cost versus value, buyers can make more informed choices, aligning their purchases with their personal preferences and expectations.

Tracking Spending

Understanding how to manage spending is an essential skill for anyone diving into the world of Amazon mystery boxes. These intriguing packages, filled with unknown treasures, can be both exciting and addictive. The allure of surprise can often lead to overspending if not approached with discipline and careful planning. It begins with setting a budget that aligns with your financial situation. Determining how much you are willing to allocate specifically for these purchases ensures that your enthusiasm remains within reasonable limits.

Maintaining a detailed record of every purchase is crucial. This process involves noting down the cost of each mystery box, the date of purchase, and any additional expenses such as shipping or handling fees. By regularly updating this log, you create a transparent view of your spending habits, making it easier to identify patterns or tendencies that might need adjustment. This log not only helps in tracking expenses but also serves as a reflection of the value derived from each box.

Utilizing digital tools can significantly enhance the tracking process. Numerous apps and software are designed to monitor spending, offering features that categorize expenses and generate insightful reports. Incorporating these tools into your routine can automate the tracking process, providing a clear overview of your spending habits over time. These digital solutions can alert you when you approach your monthly budget, helping to prevent impulsive purchases.

It's also beneficial to periodically review your spending habits. Setting aside time each month to assess your purchases allows you to evaluate whether the mystery boxes are delivering the excitement and value you anticipated. This reflection can lead to more informed decisions about future purchases. Consider the contents of the boxes you have received and whether they met your expectations in terms of quality and novelty. This assessment can guide your future buying strategies, helping you decide which sellers or types of boxes are worth your investment.

Engaging with online communities can provide additional insights into managing spending effectively. Forums and social media groups dedicated to mystery box enthusiasts often share tips on budgeting and tracking expenses. These platforms can offer advice on identifying reputable sellers, finding the best deals, and avoiding common pitfalls that lead to unnecessary spending. Participating in these discussions can broaden your understanding and enhance your ability to make informed purchasing decisions.

Lastly, maintaining a balance between indulgence and restraint is key. While the thrill of discovery is a significant aspect of purchasing mystery boxes, it is important to remain mindful of the financial implications. Establishing a clear understanding of your spending limits, coupled with disciplined tracking and periodic reviews, will ensure that your experience remains enjoyable and financially sustainable. By adopting these strategies, you can continue to explore the captivating world of Amazon mystery boxes without compromising your financial well-being.

Maximizing Value

In the world of Amazon mystery boxes, unearthing treasures requires a keen eye and a strategic approach. The allure of these boxes lies in their unpredictability, offering a tantalizing mix of excitement and risk. To truly maximize the value from each purchase, one must adopt a methodical mindset, balancing the thrill of the unknown with calculated decision-making.

First, understanding the types of boxes available is crucial. Mystery boxes vary widely in content, ranging from electronics and gadgets to fashion and home goods. Identifying your interests and aligning them with the category of the box increases the likelihood of finding items that hold personal or resale value. Researching sellers and reading reviews can provide insights into the quality and reliability of the boxes on offer, ensuring you make informed decisions.

Budget management plays a pivotal role in maximizing value. Setting a clear budget helps avoid overspending and allows for a more focused approach when selecting boxes. Consider allocating funds across multiple boxes rather than investing heavily in a single purchase. This strategy diversifies potential returns and reduces the risk associated with any one box containing less valuable items.

Another important aspect is leveraging online communities and forums dedicated to mystery box enthusiasts. These platforms are treasure troves of information, offering tips, unboxing experiences, and recommendations. Engaging with these communities can enhance your understanding of market trends and consumer experiences, guiding your purchasing decisions.

Additionally, patience is a virtue when it comes to extracting maximum value. Often, the contents of a mystery box may not immediately reveal their worth. Conducting thorough research on the items received, including their market value and demand, can uncover hidden gems that may not have been apparent at first glance. This diligence can transform seemingly mundane items into profitable assets.

Reselling is another avenue to explore for maximizing value. Platforms such as eBay, Facebook Marketplace, and specialized resale sites offer opportunities to sell unwanted or less interesting items. Crafting compelling listings with clear photographs and detailed descriptions can attract potential buyers and help recoup or even exceed the initial investment. Understanding market demand and timing your sales can further enhance profitability.

Networking with other buyers can also yield benefits. Sharing experiences and trading items with fellow enthusiasts can lead to mutually beneficial exchanges, expanding your collection or returning value to your investment. Building relationships within the community fosters a collaborative environment where tips and insights are freely shared.

Lastly, maintaining a sense of adventure and experimentation is key. While strategic planning is essential, the joy of mystery boxes lies in their unpredictability. Embrace the surprises, learn from each purchase, and refine your approach over time. This balance of strategy and spontaneity not only enhances the experience but also increases the potential for discovering true value within the hidden confines of Amazon's mystery offerings.

CHAPTER 6:

MAKING THE PURCHASE

Navigating the world of Amazon Mystery Boxes is akin to embarking on a thrilling treasure hunt. The anticipation of uncovering hidden gems, or perhaps amusing oddities, begins with the simple yet exhilarating step of placing an order. This initial action is not just a transaction; it is the gateway to an experience filled with curiosity and surprise.

To begin, one must first immerse themselves in the digital marketplace, where a myriad of options awaits. The Amazon platform, with its endless array of choices, serves as the perfect stage for this adventure. As you enter the virtual realm, a quick search for 'Mystery Boxes' reveals a colorful tapestry of possibilities, each box promising an unknown assortment of items. The excitement builds as you scroll through the offerings, each thumbnail a potential Pandora's box.

The choices are vast, ranging from themed boxes, like electronics or fashion, to more generalized assortments. Carefully crafted descriptions accompany each listing, hinting at the potential contents and sparking the imagination. Some boxes boast the allure of high-value items, while others promise quirky novelties that add a touch of whimsy to the experience. It's important to take note of seller ratings and reviews, as they offer valuable insights into the reliability and satisfaction of previous buyers.

Once a decision is made, the process of placing an order is straightforward yet satisfying. Selecting the desired mystery box is akin to choosing a sealed envelope from a stack, each one holding its own secrets. With a simple click, the item is added to your cart, and the journey begins. The checkout process, a familiar dance of clicks and confirmations, leads you through payment options and shipping details. Here, the anticipation is palpable, as each step brings you closer to the moment of revelation.

Before finalizing the purchase, double-check the delivery address and payment information, ensuring that no detail is overlooked. The thrill of the unknown is best enjoyed when logistical concerns are seamlessly managed. Once confirmed, an order confirmation email lands in your inbox, a digital receipt of your impending adventure.

With the order placed, a sense of eager anticipation takes hold. The waiting period, although brief, is filled with daydreams of what might arrive. Will it be a collection of gadgets, a bundle of fashion accessories, or perhaps something entirely unexpected? The beauty of the mystery box lies in its unpredictability, a reminder of the simple joys of surprise.

As the delivery date approaches, excitement mounts. The doorbell ringing signals the arrival of your mystery box, a tangible manifestation of the adventure you initiated with a single click. The act of placing an order, though seemingly mundane, is the first step in a narrative of discovery, where the unknown becomes a source of delight and curiosity. The anticipation of unveiling the contents is a testament to the allure of mystery boxes, a modern-day treasure chest waiting to be explored.

Payment Methods

When venturing into the world of Amazon mystery boxes, understanding the variety of payment methods available is crucial to ensuring a smooth and secure transaction. Each method offers its own unique set of benefits and potential drawbacks, making it important for buyers to choose the one that best suits their needs and preferences.

Credit and debit cards remain the most popular payment options for purchasing Amazon mystery boxes. These cards are widely accepted due to their convenience and the added layer of security they offer through fraud protection features. Most major credit card companies provide their customers with insurance on purchases, which can be particularly reassuring when dealing with the uncertain nature of mystery boxes. Additionally, using these cards can sometimes offer rewards, such as cashback or points, which can be accumulated for future purchases.

Another widely used method is the Amazon Gift Card. These cards can be purchased in various denominations and are ideal for those who prefer not to use their personal banking information online. Amazon Gift Cards can be an excellent choice for gift-givers who want to introduce friends or family members to the thrill of mystery boxes, as they allow recipients to choose the items that intrigue them the most without incurring any personal expense.

For those who prioritize privacy and security, digital wallets like PayPal, Apple Pay, and Google Pay offer a modern solution. These platforms act as intermediaries between the buyer and the seller, ensuring that sensitive financial information is not directly shared with the merchant. Digital wallets are particularly appealing to tech-savvy buyers who appreciate the ease of use and quick transaction times associated with these platforms.

Some buyers may also consider using alternative payment methods such as cryptocurrency. While not as mainstream as traditional payment options, using cryptocurrency can offer anonymity and a level of security that appeals to those wary of sharing personal information online. However, it's important to note that not all sellers accept cryptocurrency, so buyers should verify payment acceptance before proceeding with their purchase.

Amazon Pay is another convenient option for those who frequently shop on Amazon. By using Amazon Pay, buyers can streamline the checkout process by using the payment information already stored in their Amazon account. This method not only saves time but also offers the same level of security and customer service that users expect from Amazon.

Buyers should always be mindful of potential fees associated with different payment methods. Some credit cards may charge foreign transaction fees if the seller is located outside the buyer's home country. Additionally, digital wallet platforms may impose their own transaction fees, which could impact the overall cost of purchasing a mystery box.

By carefully considering the available payment methods and selecting the one that aligns with their priorities, buyers can enhance their overall shopping experience. Whether prioritizing security, convenience, or rewards, understanding the nuances of each payment option allows for informed decision-making, ultimately leading to a more satisfying journey into the mysterious world of Amazon mystery boxes.

Shipping Considerations

As you delve into the world of Amazon mystery boxes, one aspect that requires careful attention is the shipping process. The anticipation of receiving a box filled with unknown treasures can be thrilling, but understanding the intricacies of shipping can significantly enhance this experience. When purchasing these enigmatic packages, the details surrounding their journey from seller to doorstep are as varied as the contents themselves.

Firstly, consider the origin of the mystery box. Boxes sourced from international sellers may take longer to arrive compared to those shipped domestically. The geographical distance, coupled with customs procedures, can add several days, if not weeks, to the expected delivery time. It's important to check whether the seller provides tracking information, as this can offer peace of mind and allow you to monitor the progress of your package.

Shipping costs are another crucial factor. Some sellers incorporate shipping fees into the total price of the mystery box, while others list them separately. It's wise to compare these costs across different sellers to ensure you're getting the best deal. Additionally, be aware of any potential hidden charges, such as customs duties or taxes, which can sometimes be an unwelcome surprise upon delivery.

The packaging of the mystery box also warrants consideration. A well-packaged box not only protects its contents during transit but also adds to the excitement of the unboxing experience. Sellers who take pride in their packaging often provide detailed descriptions or images, allowing you to gauge the level of care taken in preparing the box. Bubble wrap, sturdy cardboard, and other protective materials are indicators of a seller who values customer satisfaction.

Furthermore, the reputation of the shipping carrier plays a pivotal role in the delivery process. Established carriers with a track record of reliability can offer more assurance that your mystery box will arrive safely and on time. In contrast, lesser-known carriers might pose a risk of delays or damage. Customer reviews can provide insights into which carriers are most dependable.

Lastly, the timing of your purchase can influence the shipping experience. During peak shopping seasons, such as holidays or major sales events, shipping networks can become congested, leading to potential delays. Planning your purchase outside of these busy periods might result in a smoother delivery process.

In essence, while the allure of Amazon mystery boxes lies in their unpredictability, applying a strategic approach to shipping considerations can enhance the overall experience. By meticulously evaluating factors such as origin, costs, packaging, carrier reliability, and timing, you can ensure that the anticipation of your mystery box culminates in a satisfying and seamless unboxing adventure.

Dealing with Delays

In the world of Amazon mystery boxes, anticipation is part of the thrill. The moment you click 'buy,' a wave of excitement courses through you, fueled by the promise of unknown treasures that could soon be yours. Yet, as with any online purchase, delays can occur, turning that excitement into a test of patience. Understanding how to effectively handle these delays can make the difference between a frustrating experience and a manageable waiting period.

When you first encounter a delay, it's essential to maintain a calm demeanor. Delays can occur for various reasons, such as logistical issues, weather conditions, or increased demand. Recognizing that these factors are often beyond your control is the first step in dealing with the situation. Instead of letting frustration take over, use this time to further engage with the mystery box community. Online forums and social media groups dedicated to mystery box enthusiasts are excellent platforms to share your experiences and gather insights from others who might be facing similar situations.

Communication is key when dealing with delays. Stay informed by regularly checking your order status through your Amazon account. If the delay extends beyond the estimated delivery date without any updates, don't hesitate to reach out to Amazon's customer service. They can provide you with the latest information regarding your shipment and may offer solutions, such as refunds or credits, if the delay becomes excessively long. Maintaining a polite and patient tone during these interactions can often yield better results, as customer service representatives are more likely to assist a courteous customer.

While waiting, consider exploring other aspects of the Amazon mystery box experience. Use this time to research different types of boxes available and read reviews from other buyers. This can help you make informed decisions for future purchases and keep your excitement alive. You might even discover new sellers or unique box themes that pique your interest, thus expanding your mystery box journey.

Additionally, delays can serve as an opportunity to manage your expectations. The unpredictable nature of mystery boxes means that not every item will be a hit. Use the waiting period to remind yourself of the adventurous spirit that attracted you to mystery boxes in the first place. This mindset can help mitigate potential disappointment and keep the experience enjoyable, regardless of the outcome.

Engaging in related hobbies or activities can also be a productive way to pass the time. Perhaps you've always wanted to start a collection of some kind, or maybe there's a DIY project you've been meaning to tackle. Channeling your anticipation into creative pursuits can be a rewarding distraction and may even enhance your appreciation for the items you eventually receive.

In the grand scheme of things, delays are a minor setback in the thrilling world of mystery boxes. By approaching them with patience, communication, and a touch of creativity, you can turn an inconvenient wait into an opportunity for growth and exploration. With each delay, you not only become a more seasoned mystery box buyer but also cultivate a deeper appreciation for the surprises that await you.

CHAPTER 7:

THE UNBOXING EXPEREINCE

The thrill of the unknown can be a powerful force, stirring a sense of wonder and curiosity that is nearly impossible to resist. As one stands on the brink of purchasing an Amazon mystery box, a whirlwind of emotions begins to unfurl. It's a unique blend of anticipation and excitement, akin to the moments before unwrapping a long-awaited gift. Each box, sealed and unassuming, holds within it the promise of surprise and discovery. The possibilities are endless, and it is this uncertainty that fuels the imagination.

Picture the scene: a nondescript cardboard box arrives, its exterior giving no hint of the treasures it might contain. The weight of it in your hands sends a jolt of exhilaration through your veins. Is it heavy with gadgets, or light as a feather, suggesting delicate trinkets or perhaps something entirely unexpected? The tactile experience of holding the box, feeling its contours, and hearing any subtle noises within, adds an extra layer to the sensory anticipation.

As you cut through the packing tape, an electric sense of suspense fills the air. The moment before the box is opened is filled with infinite possibilities. Will it be filled with items of great value, or will it contain peculiar oddities that ignite your curiosity even further? This is the magic of the mystery box—its contents are a secret until the final reveal.

The allure of these mystery boxes lies in the adventure they promise. Each purchase is a gamble, a leap into the unknown, where the payoff is not just the physical items you receive, but the experience itself. It's a form of entertainment, a game of chance that appeals to the adventurer within. The anticipation builds as you imagine the stories behind each item, their origins, and the journey they took to arrive at your doorstep.

Moreover, the social aspect of mystery boxes cannot be ignored. Sharing the experience with friends, family, or even a wider audience online can amplify the excitement. There is a communal joy in witnessing the unveiling of the contents, in sharing the surprise and delight with others. This shared experience can transform a solitary moment into a collective adventure, where each person brings their own interpretation and reaction to the table.

Mystery boxes also tap into a deeper psychological need for novelty and surprise. In a world where so much is predictable and routine, the unexpected nature of these boxes offers a refreshing break from the norm. They provide a safe space for exploration, where the stakes are low, but the potential for delight is high.

In essence, the act of purchasing an Amazon mystery box is not just about acquiring new items, but about embracing the unknown and the emotions it stirs. It's about indulging in the excitement of discovery and the anticipation of what lies beneath the surface. Each box is a vessel of potential, waiting to be unlocked, and the journey to uncover its secrets is as thrilling as the items themselves. The anticipation and excitement are not just byproducts of the experience; they are at its very heart.

Recording Your Unboxing

Capturing the moment of unveiling your Amazon Mystery Box is an art that blends anticipation with technology, turning a simple act into a memorable spectacle. As the heart races with excitement, setting up for the recording becomes a ritual, each step carefully orchestrated to ensure the magic of the moment is preserved in its entirety. Begin by selecting the perfect setting, one that complements the mystery of the box without overshadowing it. A well-lit room is essential, where natural light dances across surfaces, illuminating the contents as they are revealed. Artificial lighting can serve as an auxiliary, casting a soft glow that highlights the box and its treasures.

Positioning the camera is the next critical step. The angle should be wide enough to capture your reactions, yet focused enough to showcase the box and its contents. A tripod can be invaluable here, providing stability and freeing your hands to explore the contents with ease. Consider the background – it should be uncluttered, allowing the viewer's attention to remain on the unfolding drama of the unboxing.

Sound quality is often overlooked but plays a vital role in the recording. Ensure the room is quiet, free from distractions that could detract from the experience. A good microphone can capture the subtle sounds – the rustle of tissue paper, the gentle thud of an item as it is placed on the table, and the excitement in your voice as each mystery is revealed.

Before pressing record, take a moment to compose yourself. This is your moment of discovery, and your genuine reactions are what will resonate with viewers. Whether it's a gasp of surprise or a chuckle of amusement, authenticity is key. As you begin, narrate the process, sharing your thoughts and feelings. This personal touch transforms the recording from a mere visual document into a shared experience.

As each item emerges from the box, take time to appreciate it. Describe its texture, color, and potential uses, inviting viewers to engage with the mystery alongside you. Hold each item up to the camera, allowing it to fill the frame and capture its details. This attention to detail not only showcases the items but also enhances the viewer's connection to the unboxing.

Editing the recording is where the magic truly happens. Trim unnecessary footage to maintain a dynamic pace, yet ensure the essence of the experience remains intact. Add captions or annotations if needed, providing additional context or information about the items. Background music can enhance the mood, but it should be subtle, never overpowering the narrative.

Once the recording is complete, consider the platform where it will be shared. Each platform has its nuances, and understanding these can maximize the impact of your unboxing. Whether it's the instant engagement of social media or the curated experience of a personal blog, each choice influences how your unboxing is perceived.

In the end, recording your unboxing is about more than just documenting the contents of a box. It's about capturing the thrill of discovery, creating a narrative that engages and excites, and sharing a moment of joy with the world.

Sharing on Social Media

The thrill of unboxing an Amazon mystery box is an experience that many find exhilarating. It's a moment filled with anticipation, curiosity, and a dash of suspense as you peel away the layers to reveal the unknown treasures inside. This excitement is something that many enthusiasts are eager to share with others, and social media platforms provide the perfect stage for this. Sharing your mystery box journey on social media not only allows you to connect with like-minded individuals but also lets you document your findings, reactions, and perhaps even inspire others to dive into the world of mystery boxes.

When you decide to share your mystery box experience on social media, consider which platform best suits your style and audience.

Instagram, with its visual-centric focus, is an ideal place for showcasing the aesthetics of your mystery box. Here, you can post a series of photos or a captivating video of the unboxing process. Utilize Instagram Stories or Reels to give your followers a real-time glimpse into your adventure. Adding hashtags like #AmazonMysteryBox or #UnboxingExperience can help reach a wider audience who share the same interests.

For those who prefer a more interactive approach, platforms like Facebook Live or Instagram Live offer the chance to unbox your mystery box in real-time, engaging directly with your audience as they comment and react to each item you reveal. This live interaction can create a sense of community as viewers share their excitement, guesses, and even advice on what to do with the items you unveil.

YouTube is another powerful platform for sharing your mystery box story. Creating a dedicated unboxing video allows you to delve deeper into each item, offering detailed descriptions, personal insights, and potential uses for what you find. You can even create a series of videos, each focusing on different categories of mystery boxes, providing your channel with varied content that keeps your audience coming back for more. Be sure to encourage viewers to like, subscribe, and comment, fostering a community of mystery box enthusiasts.

Twitter, while more text-focused, is perfect for quick updates and sharing immediate reactions. You can tweet about your anticipation before the box arrives, your first impressions upon opening it, and your thoughts on the contents. Engaging with other mystery box fans through Twitter chats or threads can also enhance your experience, as you exchange tips and stories with others who share your passion.

Regardless of the platform you choose, remember to engage with your audience. Respond to comments, participate in discussions, and consider their feedback when planning future unboxing content. Sharing your experiences on social media not only enhances your enjoyment of mystery boxes but also builds a community of curious adventurers eager to explore the unknown together. Through these interactions, you might even discover new types of mystery boxes to try, keeping the adventure alive and ever-evolving. The world of mystery boxes is vast and varied, and your social media presence can be a beacon for others navigating this fascinating realm.

Engaging with the Community

Participating in the community of Amazon mystery box enthusiasts is akin to stepping into a vibrant bazaar where excitement, curiosity, and camaraderie are the currencies of exchange. This community, diverse yet unified by a shared intrigue for the unknown, offers a wealth of knowledge and support for both newcomers and seasoned treasure hunters alike.

Online forums and social media platforms serve as the bustling hubs of interaction, where members eagerly share their latest finds, offer advice, and swap tips on navigating the often unpredictable world of mystery box purchases. These digital spaces are rich tapestries woven with stories of spectacular discoveries and occasional disappointments, each thread contributing to a collective understanding of the art and science of purchasing these enigmatic boxes.

Within these virtual walls, the seasoned veterans of the mystery box realm often take on mentoring roles, guiding novices through the intricacies of selecting reputable sellers, deciphering reviews, and managing expectations. Their insights, forged through countless transactions and experiences, provide invaluable guidance that can help newcomers avoid common pitfalls and enhance their overall experience.

Moreover, the community often organizes events and challenges that add an extra layer of excitement to the mystery box experience. These events, ranging from unboxing competitions to themed purchasing challenges, foster a sense of belonging and healthy competition among participants. They also offer opportunities for members to showcase their creativity and strategic thinking, as they curate and present their mystery box hauls in imaginative and entertaining ways.

Beyond the digital realm, local meet-ups and swap events further solidify the bonds within the community. These gatherings provide a tangible connection, allowing members to share their passion for mystery boxes in a more personal and direct manner. Attendees often exchange items, share insights, and forge friendships that extend beyond the realm of mystery boxes, creating a network of like-minded individuals who share a love for adventure and surprise.

Engaging with the community also opens doors to exclusive deals and insider information. Members often share discount codes, alert each other to upcoming sales, and even collaborate on bulk purchases to maximize savings. This spirit of collaboration and mutual assistance underscores the community's ethos of shared success and enjoyment.

In essence, the community serves as both a resource and a refuge, offering a supportive environment where enthusiasts can freely express their passion and curiosity. It is a space where the thrill of discovery is celebrated, lessons are learned through shared experiences, and the joy of the unknown is embraced collectively. For anyone venturing into the world of Amazon mystery boxes, becoming an active member of this community can transform what might be a solitary pursuit into a shared adventure filled with learning, laughter, and lasting connections.

CHAPTER 8

ASSESSING THE CONTENTS

When you first open an Amazon mystery box, a sense of anticipation fills the air. Each box is a puzzle waiting to be solved, its contents hidden from view until the very moment you peel back the tape and lift the flaps. As the box opens, a new world of possibilities reveals itself, each item a piece of a larger story. Evaluating these items requires a discerning eye and a methodical approach, ensuring that every treasure—or potential disappointment—is given its due consideration.

Begin by taking a moment to survey the contents laid before you. The initial impression can often set the tone for your entire evaluation process. Are the items neatly packed, or does the box seem haphazardly filled? This first glance can provide clues about the care taken in curating the box. Next, focus on the individual items, one by one, as each holds its own potential value and intrigue.

The first step in evaluating an item is to assess its condition.

Look for any signs of wear and tear, such as scratches, dents, or missing parts. An item in pristine condition can often fetch a higher value, whether you plan to keep it or resell it. On the other hand, an item with visible damage might still hold value if it is rare or in high demand. For electronics, power them on, if possible, to ensure they are in working order.

Once the physical condition is assessed, turn your attention to the brand and model. Recognizable brands often carry a certain assurance of quality and desirability. Researching the specific model can provide insights into its market value and popularity. Use online resources and marketplaces to compare similar items, noting any price trends or demand fluctuations. This step is crucial in determining whether an item is a hidden gem or a common find.

Beyond the brand, consider the functionality and practicality of each item. Some items may be innovative yet impractical, while others might be mundane but extremely useful. Think about who might find value in the item, whether it is a niche market or a broader audience. This consideration not only helps in identifying potential resale avenues but also in deciding if the item might find a place in your own life.

As you evaluate each item, keep a record of your findings. Note down the condition, brand, estimated value, and any other pertinent details. This will not only help in organizing your thoughts but also in tracking your overall experience with mystery boxes over time.

Patterns may emerge, guiding future purchases and honing your skills in detecting value.

Ultimately, evaluating the items within an Amazon mystery box is as much an art as it is a science. It requires a balance of intuition, research, and a touch of luck. With each box, you become more adept at distinguishing between the mundane and the extraordinary, between potential profit and personal delight. The thrill of the unknown, combined with the potential for discovery, makes each evaluation a unique adventure in its own right.

Determining Value

Understanding the worth of an Amazon mystery box is akin to unlocking a treasure chest with an unknown fortune inside. The thrill of the unknown is what lures buyers in, but it's the potential value that keeps them coming back. To truly determine the value of a mystery box, one must first consider the various factors that contribute to its allure and potential payoff.

First, consider the source of the mystery box. Amazon mystery boxes can be sourced from different sellers, each with their own reputation and history. Some sellers are known for curating boxes that are filled with high-quality items, while others might offer boxes that are hit-or-miss. Researching the seller's past reviews and ratings can provide insight into the likelihood of receiving a valuable box. Look for sellers who have consistently positive feedback, as this suggests a history of satisfied customers and successful transactions.

Next, the size and type of the box play a significant role in its potential value. Boxes come in various sizes, from small packages to large crates, and the contents can range from electronics and gadgets to clothing and beauty products. Larger boxes might seem more appealing due to their size, but it's important to consider the type of items you are interested in. A small box filled with high-value electronics could be more worthwhile than a large box of miscellaneous items with lower resale value.

The element of randomness is another factor that influences the perceived value of a mystery box. While the contents are unknown, some sellers provide hints or themes for their boxes, such as 'tech gadgets' or 'home essentials.' These themes can help guide your expectations and align them with your personal interests. A mystery box themed around a specific category that you are passionate about is likely to hold more value for you personally, even if the monetary worth of the items varies.

Additionally, the thrill of discovery is a non-monetary value that cannot be overlooked. The excitement of unboxing and the anticipation of discovering what's inside can be a rewarding experience in itself. For many, this emotional aspect adds to the overall value of the purchase, making it worthwhile even if the items themselves do not meet high monetary expectations.

Lastly, consider the potential resale value of the items within the box. Some buyers purchase mystery boxes with the intent to resell the contents individually. This approach requires a keen eye for market trends and an understanding of what items are in demand. Analyzing the potential retail value of the items can help determine if the box is a good investment. Platforms like eBay or Amazon itself can provide insight into what similar items are selling for, allowing you to gauge the potential profit margin.

In essence, determining the value of an Amazon mystery box is a multifaceted process that involves assessing both tangible and intangible elements. By carefully considering the source, size, theme, and potential resale value, buyers can make informed decisions and enhance their overall experience.

Keeping or Returning

The anticipation of unboxing a mystery box from Amazon is akin to unwrapping a surprise gift, filled with the potential for unexpected delight or mild disappointment. As the layers of packaging are peeled away, the contents of the box reveal themselves, each item carrying its own story and possibilities. The decision to keep or return these items becomes a nuanced dance between practicality, excitement, and personal preference.

Upon opening a box, the first instinct might be to assess the immediate utility and appeal of each item. Some items might instantly spark joy or fulfill a long-standing need, making the decision to keep them almost instinctive.

Perhaps it's a gadget that fits perfectly into a tech enthusiast's collection or a piece of decor that seamlessly blends with the aesthetic of a room. These are the treasures that make the mystery box experience worthwhile, offering value beyond their monetary worth.

Conversely, there are items that might not resonate as strongly, either due to redundancy or a mismatch with personal taste. Here lies the dilemma: to keep or return. Returning items might seem like an arduous process, but Amazon's return policy is designed to be user-friendly, allowing for seamless exchanges or refunds. This ease of return can alleviate the pressure of making immediate decisions, giving buyers the freedom to experiment and explore the contents of their boxes without the fear of commitment.

The decision-making process is often influenced by factors such as the perceived value of the item, its condition, and the potential for future use. For some, the thrill of the hunt and the discovery of unique items outweighs the need for practical utility. They may choose to keep items that are quirky or unusual, viewing them as conversation pieces or collectibles. Others might prioritize functionality and opt to return items that don't serve an immediate purpose or duplicate existing possessions.

Moreover, the emotional and psychological aspects of keeping or returning cannot be overlooked. There is a certain satisfaction in keeping an item that feels like a serendipitous find, a feeling that it was 'meant to be.' On the other hand, there is also empowerment in the decision to return, knowing that one is not bound to keep items that do not bring joy or utility.

The process of keeping or returning items from a mystery box is, in essence, a reflection of personal values and lifestyle choices. It's a balancing act between the excitement of discovery and the pragmatism of decision-making. Each box opened is a journey into the unknown, offering a unique opportunity to reassess what is truly valuable and necessary. Thus, the art of deciding whether to keep or return items becomes an integral part of the mystery box experience, one that enriches the overall adventure of buying Amazon mystery boxes.

Satisfaction and Feedback

The allure of Amazon mystery boxes often lies in the suspense and excitement they bring to the recipient. As the tape is peeled back and the contents are revealed, what follows is a profound moment of anticipation that can swing between elation and disappointment. This emotional rollercoaster is an integral part of the experience, and it is here that satisfaction plays a pivotal role. Satisfaction in the context of mystery boxes is not just about the tangible items received; it is deeply intertwined with the expectations set before the box is even opened. Buyers often find themselves weighing the perceived value of the items against the price paid, and the emotional satisfaction derived from this perceived value is what ultimately defines their experience.

The feedback loop created by these experiences is crucial for both buyers and sellers. For buyers, sharing feedback is a way to voice their satisfaction or dissatisfaction, influencing future purchasing decisions. This feedback often takes the form of reviews on platforms like Amazon, where potential buyers scour the comments for insights into the likelihood of a successful purchase. Positive feedback often highlights the thrill of receiving unexpected treasures, while negative feedback may focus on unmet expectations or poor value for money.

For sellers, this feedback is invaluable. It serves as a direct line to the consumer's psyche, offering insights into what works and what doesn't. Sellers can use this information to tweak their offerings, ensuring that the mystery boxes they curate align more closely with consumer desires. This symbiotic relationship between satisfaction and feedback fosters an environment where both parties benefit; buyers enjoy a better product, and sellers enhance their reputation and sales.

The satisfaction derived from mystery boxes is also influenced by the element of surprise. Unlike traditional purchases where the buyer knows exactly what they are getting, mystery boxes rely on the unknown to generate excitement. This unpredictability can heighten satisfaction when the items exceed expectations or align with personal tastes. Conversely, it can lead to dissatisfaction if the items are perceived as mundane or irrelevant. Therefore, the art of curating a successful mystery box lies in striking a balance between surprise and value, ensuring that the contents resonate with a broad audience while still offering the thrill of discovery.

Feedback, in this context, becomes a tool for adjusting this balance. Sellers who actively engage with feedback can finetune their offerings, using constructive criticism to identify areas for improvement. This might involve adjusting the mix of items, enhancing the quality of products, or even reevaluating the themes of the boxes. By doing so, they not only increase the likelihood of satisfying their customers but also build a loyal customer base that trusts in their ability to deliver a worthwhile experience.

The interplay between satisfaction and feedback in the world of Amazon mystery boxes is a dynamic one, constantly evolving as consumer expectations shift and sellers strive to meet them. It is a dance of anticipation and response, where each party plays a crucial role in shaping the other's experience. As the mystery box phenomenon continues to grow, understanding and optimizing this relationship will be key to sustaining its appeal and ensuring that the thrill of the unknown remains a source of joy rather than disappointment.

CHAPTER 9

LEARNING FROM   EXPERIENCE

In the dimly lit room where anticipation hangs heavy in the air, a lone figure sits surrounded by an array of Amazon mystery boxes. Each box, a sealed enigma, holds the promise of surprise, delight, or perhaps the unexpected. As the individual contemplates the assortment of cardboard containers, a reflective mood takes hold, urging a pause before the eager unboxing begins.

The allure of the mystery box is undeniable, a modern treasure chest that taps into the innate human desire for discovery and the thrill of the unknown. Yet, with each purchase comes a moment of introspection. What drives the decision to acquire these enigmatic parcels? Is it the potential for valuable finds, the sheer novelty of the experience, or perhaps an escape from the mundane routine of everyday life?

As the boxes sit, waiting to reveal their secrets, there is time to consider the motivations that led to their acquisition.

The process of buying a mystery box is not merely transactional; it is an emotional journey, a dance between curiosity and caution. Each box represents a roll of the dice, a gamble where the stakes are measured in both monetary terms and emotional satisfaction.

Reflecting on past experiences with mystery boxes can offer valuable insights. Some boxes may have yielded delightful surprises, items that brought joy and utility. Others might have been less rewarding, containing objects that now gather dust or were swiftly discarded. These memories serve as a guide, shaping future purchasing decisions and tempering expectations.

The decision to buy a mystery box often begins with a spark of curiosity, a desire to explore what lies beyond the ordinary. For some, it is the thrill of the hunt, the hope of unearthing a hidden gem that fuels the purchase. For others, it is the allure of a curated surprise, a package meticulously assembled to intrigue and delight.

However, it is essential to weigh this curiosity against practicality. As one reflects on the contents of past boxes, questions arise: Were the items worth the investment? Did they bring genuine satisfaction? Or were they merely fleeting distractions, quickly forgotten? These reflections help hone a more discerning eye, guiding future purchases towards boxes that promise greater value and personal relevance.

Moreover, the act of purchasing a mystery box can be seen as a reflection of one's own values and desires. It is an opportunity to explore personal tastes and preferences, to discover new interests, and to embrace the unexpected. Each box becomes a mirror, reflecting not only the contents within but also the hopes and aspirations of the buyer.

In this quiet moment of reflection, surrounded by the silent anticipation of unopened boxes, there is a realization that the true value of a mystery box extends beyond its physical contents. It lies in the experience itself, the stories that unfold with each reveal, and the personal journey of discovery and self-awareness that accompanies the act of unboxing. As hands hover over the first box, ready to break the seal, there is a sense of readiness, a thoughtful acknowledgment of the past and a hopeful gaze towards the future.

Improving Future Buys

To refine the art of acquiring Amazon mystery boxes, one must delve into a blend of strategy, research, and intuition. It's about transforming each purchase into a learning experience that enhances future selections. The initial step involves thoroughly analyzing past acquisitions. Reflect on the contents of previous boxes, assessing both the valuable items and the less impressive ones. This reflection provides insight into patterns and trends that may influence your next choice.

Consider maintaining a detailed record of your purchases, noting the seller, the type of box, the cost, and a brief inventory of the contents. This log becomes an invaluable tool as it allows you to identify which sellers consistently offer higher quality items and which types of boxes align with your interests or needs. Over time, these records reveal patterns, helping you make more informed decisions.

Engage with online communities and forums dedicated to mystery box enthusiasts. These platforms are treasure troves of shared experiences, tips, and warnings. By participating in discussions, you gain access to a wealth of collective knowledge. Fellow enthusiasts often share their successes and disappointments, which can guide you in selecting reputable sellers or avoiding potential pitfalls.

Additionally, these communities might offer recommendations for sellers who are known for curating boxes with high-value items.

When browsing potential purchases, pay close attention to seller ratings and reviews. A seller with consistent positive feedback is more likely to provide boxes that meet or exceed expectations. However, be wary of reviews that seem overly positive or generic, as they might not be entirely genuine. Aim to find reviews that offer specific details about the contents and condition of the items received. These insights can be more telling than star ratings alone.

Experimentation remains a crucial element in the process. While it is tempting to stick with what has been known to work, branching out to new sellers or different types of boxes can lead to unexpected rewards. Allocating a portion of your budget to explore these new options can diversify your experience and potentially uncover hidden gems.

Moreover, developing a keen sense of timing can significantly influence the outcome of your purchases. Some sellers might release boxes that coincide with particular seasons or events, which can result in thematic or special edition items. Being aware of these opportunities allows you to capitalize on unique offerings that might not be available at other times.

Lastly, trust your instincts. While data and research are invaluable, there is an element of intuition in selecting a mystery box. If a particular listing captures your attention or feels promising, it might be worth pursuing. Balancing analytical thinking with a touch of gut feeling can lead to satisfying and successful acquisitions.

By integrating these practices, each purchase becomes an opportunity for growth and discovery. The excitement of the unknown is coupled with a strategic approach, turning the acquisition of Amazon mystery boxes into a refined and rewarding hobby.

Recognizing Patterns

Navigating the world of Amazon mystery boxes can initially seem like a daunting task, with an overwhelming variety of options and unpredictable contents. However, with careful observation and keen insight, one can begin to recognize patterns that lead to more successful and satisfying purchases. The ability to discern these patterns often separates the novice from the seasoned mystery box enthusiast.

When approaching the task of identifying patterns, the first step involves examining the seller's history and reputation. Sellers with a consistently high rating and positive reviews are more likely to deliver quality mystery boxes. It's important to note how frequently a seller updates their listings or introduces new boxes. Sellers who regularly refresh their offerings may have better access to new and interesting stock, which could increase the chances of receiving valuable items.

Another critical aspect is the description provided for each mystery box. While the very nature of these boxes is to maintain an element of surprise, some sellers drop subtle hints about the contents. Analyzing the language used in the descriptions can offer insights into what might be expected. For instance, if a seller frequently uses terms like "electronics," "collectibles," or "fashion," it may indicate a tendency towards including items from these categories. Over time, buyers can learn to interpret these clues to predict the general nature of the contents, thus aligning their purchases with their interests.

Price is another significant factor that often reveals patterns. Boxes priced at a premium usually promise higher-quality or more valuable items. However, this is not always a guarantee. Observing the pricing trends of different sellers over time can unveil patterns in pricing strategies and value delivery. Some sellers might offer occasional discounts or bundle deals, which can be advantageous for buyers who are vigilant and ready to seize these opportunities.

Customer reviews and unboxing videos available online are invaluable resources for recognizing patterns. These reviews often include detailed accounts of the box contents and the overall satisfaction of previous buyers. Paying attention to recurring themes in these reviews can provide a clearer picture of what to expect. Additionally, unboxing videos serve as a visual testament to the box's contents, offering yet another layer of insight into potential patterns.

Lastly, seasonal trends can influence the contents of mystery boxes. During holidays or special occasions, sellers may curate boxes with themed items or limited edition products. Recognizing these seasonal patterns allows buyers to time their purchases strategically, potentially acquiring exclusive or rare items.

In essence, recognizing patterns in the realm of Amazon mystery boxes requires a combination of research, observation, and intuition. By meticulously analyzing seller behavior, product descriptions, pricing strategies, and customer feedback, buyers can enhance their chances of making gratifying purchases. Over time, these patterns become more apparent, transforming the mystery box buying experience from a mere gamble into a skillful pursuit.

Building a Strategy

Acquiring Amazon mystery boxes is an art that requires a well-thought-out strategy. The allure of these boxes lies in their unpredictability, where the contents remain a mystery until unveiled. To maximize the thrill and potential value of these purchases, a strategic approach is indispensable. The first step in developing an effective strategy is research. Understanding the types of mystery boxes available on Amazon is crucial. Some boxes are curated by third-party sellers, while others may be returns or overstock items. Each type carries different expectations and potential rewards. Familiarizing oneself with seller ratings and reviews can provide insights into the reliability and quality of the offerings, helping to avoid disappointment.

Budgeting is another critical component. Setting a clear budget helps in managing expectations and financial risk. Mystery boxes can range from a few dollars to several hundred, depending on the perceived value of their contents. It's essential to define how much one is willing to spend on the thrill of the unknown. This budget should account for both the potential rewards and the possibility of receiving items of lesser value.

Timing plays a significant role in building a strategy.
Monitoring sales events, such as Black Friday or Cyber Monday, can lead to finding mystery boxes at discounted prices. Additionally, being aware of restock times or when sellers typically update their listings can provide an advantage, as these boxes often sell out quickly due to their popularity.

A strategic approach also involves diversification. Rather than investing heavily in a single box, spreading purchases across different sellers or categories can increase the chances of uncovering valuable items. This approach mitigates risk by not relying solely on one box to deliver high returns.

Communication with sellers can enhance the buying experience. Engaging with sellers to inquire about the nature of the contents or any specific themes can provide additional context, aiding in decision-making. Some sellers might offer clues or hints about the box contents, which can be valuable for those seeking specific types of items.

Furthermore, keeping track of past purchases can inform future buying decisions. Maintaining a record of what has been received, along with the quality and value of those items, can help refine the strategy over time. Analyzing this data allows buyers to identify patterns or sellers that consistently deliver desirable products.

Lastly, staying informed about community discussions or forums dedicated to mystery box unboxings can offer insights and tips from fellow enthusiasts. These communities often share experiences and recommendations, providing a wealth of knowledge that can enhance one's strategy.

In essence, the key to successfully purchasing Amazon mystery boxes lies in a balanced strategy that combines research, budgeting, timing, diversification, communication, and learning from past experiences. By meticulously planning each step, the thrill of the unknown can be transformed into a rewarding adventure, where surprises are met with anticipation and excitement.

CHAPTER 10

AVOIDING COMMON PITFALLS

In the thrilling world of Amazon mystery boxes, where the promise of surprise and excitement beckons, it is crucial to navigate carefully to avoid falling prey to scams. The allure of a treasure trove of unknown goods is undeniably compelling, yet it also provides fertile ground for unscrupulous individuals to exploit eager buyers. Recognizing scams in this burgeoning market requires a discerning eye and a cautious approach.

One of the most apparent red flags is an offer that seems too good to be true. Scammers often lure potential victims with the promise of high-value items at a fraction of their worth. These enticing deals are designed to cloud judgment and trigger impulsive purchases. It is essential to remember that legitimate sellers need to cover their costs and make a profit, so offers that appear disproportionately generous should be scrutinized.

Additionally, the reputation of the seller is a critical factor in distinguishing scams from genuine opportunities. Established and reputable sellers typically have a track record of positive reviews and customer feedback. It is advisable to conduct thorough research on the seller, examining their ratings and reading reviews from other buyers. Sellers with little to no history or those with predominantly negative feedback should be approached with caution.

Another common tactic employed by scammers is the use of vague or misleading product descriptions. Legitimate sellers provide clear and detailed information about the contents of their mystery boxes, even if the exact items remain undisclosed. Descriptions that are overly ambiguous or that lack essential details can be indicative of a scam. Potential buyers should be wary of listings that offer little more than generic promises of value without substantiating what that value might entail.

Payment methods also play a significant role in identifying scams. Trusted platforms generally offer secure payment options that include buyer protection, such as credit card transactions or reputable online payment services. Scammers, however, may insist on less secure methods, such as wire transfers or cryptocurrency payments, which offer little recourse for buyers if the transaction goes awry. It is advisable to avoid sellers who push for these insecure payment options.

Furthermore, communication with the seller can provide valuable insights into their legitimacy. Genuine sellers are typically transparent and responsive, willing to answer questions and provide additional information when requested. A lack of communication or evasive responses can be a warning sign of a potential scam. Buyers should trust their instincts and consider any reluctance to engage openly as a signal to proceed with caution.

The world of Amazon mystery boxes promises excitement and the thrill of the unknown, but it is essential to approach each purchase with vigilance. By recognizing the hallmarks of scams, such as unrealistic offers, dubious seller reputations, ambiguous descriptions, insecure payment methods, and poor communication, buyers can protect themselves and ensure that their foray into this intriguing market is both safe and rewarding. The ability to discern genuine opportunities from deceitful schemes is a valuable skill that will serve any mystery box enthusiast well.

Managing Expectations

When venturing into the world of Amazon mystery boxes, it's crucial to establish a clear understanding of what these enigmatic packages can offer. The allure of the unknown can be enticing, but it is essential to manage one's expectations to ensure a satisfying experience. Each mystery box is a Pandora's box of potential delights and disappointments, and navigating this realm requires a balanced approach.

Firstly, it is important to recognize that the contents of a mystery box are, by nature, unpredictable. The thrill of discovery lies in the surprise, but this also means that there is no guarantee of receiving high-value or desired items. While some may contain hidden gems, others might include items that are less appealing or useful. This unpredictability is part of the charm but can also lead to dissatisfaction if expectations are not set appropriately.

To mitigate the risk of disappointment, prospective buyers should consider the price point of the mystery box. Generally, spending within a comfortable budget is advisable since the value of the contents may not always equate to the amount spent. Understanding that the purchase is as much about the experience as it is about the physical items can help in appreciating whatever the box may hold.

Researching the seller is another critical step in managing expectations. Reviews and ratings can provide insight into the typical quality and variety of items included in their mystery boxes. Sellers with consistently positive feedback are more likely to offer boxes that meet or exceed customer expectations. However, even reputable sellers cannot guarantee specific items, so maintaining realistic expectations is still important.

Additionally, consider the theme or category of the mystery box when managing expectations. Boxes that are themed around specific interests or hobbies may have a higher likelihood of containing items that align with the buyer's preferences. For example, a mystery box labeled for technology enthusiasts might include gadgets or accessories, whereas a box themed for beauty products may contain cosmetics or skincare items. Understanding the general theme can help in setting expectations regarding the type of items that might be received.

Lastly, it's beneficial to approach the purchase with an open mind and a sense of adventure. The essence of a mystery box is the surprise element, and embracing this uncertainty can enhance the overall experience. Treating the unboxing as a fun activity rather than a transaction ensures that even if the contents are not as anticipated, the process itself can still be enjoyable.

In summary, managing expectations is a vital aspect of buying Amazon mystery boxes. By acknowledging the inherent unpredictability, setting a reasonable budget, researching sellers, considering themed boxes, and maintaining an open-minded attitude, buyers can maximize their enjoyment and minimize potential disappointment. The key is to relish the mystery for what it is—a delightful exploration into the unknown.

Handling Disappointments

In the world of Amazon mystery boxes, the thrill of anticipation is often accompanied by the sting of disappointment. As the seal of the box is broken and its contents revealed, the reality may not always align with one's expectations. This is a common experience, and understanding how to handle such disappointments can enhance the overall experience of buying these enigmatic parcels.

The first step in managing disappointment is adjusting expectations. Each mystery box is a gamble; the allure lies in the unknown, the possibility of uncovering a hidden treasure. However, not every box will contain items of high value or personal interest. Approaching each purchase with an open mind and a sense of curiosity rather than a fixed expectation can mitigate feelings of dissatisfaction. It's helpful to view each box as part of a larger adventure, where not every chapter is a climactic revelation.

When disappointment does occur, it's important to reflect on the reasons behind the purchase. Was it for the thrill of the unknown, the potential for high-value items, or simply for entertainment? Revisiting these motivations can provide perspective and lessen the impact of a less-than-exciting reveal. For some, the joy is in the unboxing itself, the moment of discovery, rather than the contents. Focusing on the experience rather than the outcome can transform disappointment into a more neutral or even positive experience.

Another strategy is to find value in unexpected ways. Sometimes, items that initially seem disappointing can be repurposed or gifted, offering joy to someone else or finding a new use in an unexpected context. This creative approach can turn a seemingly negative outcome into an opportunity for innovation and sharing. Additionally, engaging with communities of fellow mystery box enthusiasts can provide support and solace. Sharing experiences, both positive and negative, fosters a sense of camaraderie and understanding that can alleviate feelings of disappointment.

Learning from each experience is crucial. Take note of which types of boxes tend to meet personal expectations and which do not. This knowledge can inform future purchases and help refine the selection process. Over time, patterns may emerge that guide more successful and satisfying choices. Additionally, researching sellers and reading reviews can provide insight into the potential contents of a box, helping to set more realistic expectations.

Ultimately, the key to handling disappointment lies in maintaining a balanced perspective. The nature of mystery boxes inherently involves risk, and with risk comes the possibility of both reward and letdown. Embracing this duality, while focusing on the enjoyment of the process, can transform the experience into one of learning and exploration rather than one of frustration. By cultivating a mindset that values the journey over the destination, the disappointments encountered along the way can be seen as integral parts of the broader adventure of collecting Amazon mystery boxes.

Staying Informed

In the ever-evolving world of online shopping, particularly when diving into the realm of Amazon mystery boxes, staying informed is crucial. This niche market, filled with allure and the promise of surprise, requires a keen eye and a vigilant approach to keep abreast of the latest trends and potential pitfalls. Information is your ally, guiding you through the myriad of choices and ensuring that your purchases are both satisfying and safe.

The first step in staying informed is understanding the market dynamics. Amazon mystery boxes come in various forms, from electronics and fashion to home goods and collectibles. Each category has its own trends, with certain items gaining popularity due to seasonal demand or viral social media trends. Keeping an eye on these shifts can help you make informed decisions about which mystery boxes to purchase. Following relevant blogs, forums, and social media groups dedicated to mystery boxes can provide insights into what's currently in demand and which sellers are reputable.

Furthermore, subscribing to newsletters from trusted sources can be invaluable. These often include reviews of recent mystery box purchases, highlighting both the hits and the misses. Such reviews can save you from potential disappointment by steering you away from poorly rated boxes or sellers. Additionally, these sources may offer exclusive discounts or early access to popular boxes, enhancing your buying experience.

Another aspect of staying informed is understanding the legal and safety considerations involved in purchasing mystery boxes. It's essential to research and comprehend the terms and conditions associated with these purchases. Knowing the return policies, warranty details, and consumer rights can protect you from scams or unsatisfactory transactions. Engaging with consumer protection websites or forums can also keep you updated on any known issues or warnings related to specific sellers or types of mystery boxes.

Staying informed also involves being aware of the technological tools at your disposal. Price tracking tools and browser extensions can alert you to price drops or special promotions on mystery boxes, ensuring you get the best deal possible. These tools can also help you track the popularity and availability of certain boxes, giving you an edge in the competitive world of online shopping.

Lastly, networking with fellow enthusiasts can be a rich source of information. Participating in online communities or attending events dedicated to mystery boxes can provide firsthand accounts and recommendations. These interactions not only keep you informed about the latest trends but also create a sense of camaraderie and shared experience that enhances the overall enjoyment of collecting mystery boxes.

In a market as dynamic as this, information is power. By staying informed, you equip yourself with the knowledge needed to navigate the complexities of Amazon mystery boxes, ensuring that each purchase is a delightful discovery rather than a regrettable gamble. Whether it's through online research, community engagement, or utilizing technology, being informed helps you make the most of your mystery box adventures.

CHAPTER 11

THE COMMUNITY AND CULTURE

In the ever-evolving world of online marketplaces, the allure of Amazon mystery boxes has captivated the imagination of many. These enigmatic packages offer a thrill akin to a treasure hunt, promising an assortment of unknown items that could range from the mundane to the extraordinary. To navigate this intriguing landscape, joining online groups dedicated to Amazon mystery boxes becomes an essential step for both novices and seasoned enthusiasts alike. These communities serve as vibrant hubs of information, sharing insights, experiences, and tips that can significantly enhance your mystery box journey.

As you venture into these online groups, the atmosphere is one of anticipation and camaraderie. Members, bound by a shared curiosity, eagerly exchange stories of their latest acquisitions. Posts often feature detailed unboxings, with photos and videos capturing every moment of discovery. The excitement is palpable as users reveal the contents of their boxes, sometimes striking gold with high-value items, and other times encountering the quirkiness of unexpected finds. This blend of unpredictability and potential reward fuels the community's enthusiasm, encouraging a continuous cycle of participation and engagement.

Navigating these groups, you'll encounter a wealth of knowledge that can be instrumental in making informed purchasing decisions. Veteran members generously share their expertise, offering guidance on reputable sellers, pricing strategies, and tips for maximizing the value of your mystery box experience. Discussions often delve into the nuances of box selection, with debates on whether to opt for themed boxes, electronics, toys, or general merchandise. The diversity of opinions and experiences enriches the group dynamic, providing newcomers with a comprehensive understanding of what to expect and how to approach their purchases.

The collective wisdom of these communities extends beyond mere purchasing advice. Members often engage in spirited discussions about the ethics and economics of mystery boxes, pondering the sustainability of this trend and its impact on consumer behavior. These conversations add depth to the group interactions, fostering a sense of responsibility and awareness among participants. By joining these dialogues, you not only enhance your own understanding but also contribute to the broader discourse on this intriguing phenomenon.

Moreover, these online groups offer a sense of belonging and shared excitement that transcends geographical boundaries. Participants hail from various corners of the globe, each bringing unique perspectives and experiences. This diversity enriches the community, allowing for a crosspollination of ideas and fostering a spirit of inclusivity. Whether you are a seasoned collector or a curious newcomer, these groups provide a welcoming environment where your passion for Amazon mystery boxes can flourish.

In the digital age, where connections are often forged through screens, these online groups stand as a testament to the power of shared interests in creating vibrant communities. By joining these networks, you gain access to a treasure trove of information, support, and camaraderie that can significantly enhance your Amazon mystery box experience. As you immerse yourself in this world of mystery and discovery, you become part of a dynamic tapestry of individuals united by the thrill of the unknown.

Participating in Discussions

Engaging in discussions about Amazon mystery boxes offers a unique avenue to deepen one's understanding and enrich the buying experience. Within various online platforms, communities dedicated to these enigmatic purchases thrive, providing a space where enthusiasts and novices alike can share insights, tips, and experiences. These discussions often unfold in forums, social media groups, and dedicated threads on e-commerce sites, each buzzing with activity and filled with individuals eager to exchange knowledge.

Participating in these discussions starts with identifying the right platforms. Reddit, for instance, hosts numerous subreddits where users discuss their mystery box purchases, post unboxings, and offer advice. Similarly, Facebook groups dedicated to mystery box enthusiasts allow members to post questions, share reviews, and even warn others about potential scams. These communities are invaluable resources for anyone looking to delve deeper into the world of mystery boxes.

Once a suitable platform is found, actively engaging in conversations can lead to a wealth of information. Asking questions is a fundamental part of learning within these communities. Whether inquiring about the best sellers, the types of items typically found in boxes, or tips on ensuring a satisfactory purchase, community members are often more than willing to share their experiences. By participating in these discussions, one can gather diverse perspectives and insights that might not be readily available through other means.

Moreover, sharing personal experiences can also be beneficial. By contributing to discussions with one's own unboxing stories or reviews, an individual not only gives back to the community but also opens up opportunities for feedback and further learning. Such interactions can help refine one's approach to buying mystery boxes, leading to more informed decisions and potentially more satisfying purchases in the future.

Engagement in these discussions also often leads to discovering new trends and popular items within the mystery box market. Members frequently share updates on the latest box releases, discuss upcoming sales, and highlight limited-time offers. Staying informed about these trends can be advantageous for those looking to make strategic purchases or simply wanting to stay up-to-date with the latest in the mystery box world.

However, it's important to approach these discussions with a critical eye. Not all information shared in online communities is reliable, and opinions can vary widely. Cross-referencing information from multiple sources, checking the credibility of community members, and being wary of overly positive or negative reviews are all prudent practices to ensure the information gathered is accurate and useful.

In essence, engaging in discussions about Amazon mystery boxes is not just about gaining information; it's about becoming part of a community. This involvement can transform the solitary act of purchasing a box into a shared experience filled with anticipation, support, and camaraderie. Whether one is a seasoned collector or a curious newcomer, participating in these discussions enriches the mystery box journey, making it a more informed and enjoyable endeavor.

Sharing Experiences

The thrill of unboxing an Amazon mystery box is akin to the excitement of unwrapping presents on a festive morning. Each box, a sealed enigma, holds the potential for surprise and delight. As the cardboard flaps are pried open, the anticipation is palpable, a moment suspended in time where anything seems possible. The contents, a medley of the unexpected, are revealed one by one, each item telling its own story and sparking the imagination.

For many, the allure of these boxes lies not only in the mystery of their contents but also in the shared experiences they foster. Enthusiasts often gather in online forums, eager to recount their latest finds. Stories of rare collectibles, quirky gadgets, and even everyday necessities abound, each narrative adding to the collective tapestry of shared discovery. These digital spaces become a haven for camaraderie, where like-minded individuals connect over their mutual love for the unknown.

It is not uncommon to find detailed accounts of unboxing experiences, complete with photographs and videos, allowing others to partake in the joy vicariously. The community thrives on these shared moments, each post a snapshot of a unique journey into the uncharted territories of consumer goods. Some narrators have a knack for storytelling, weaving their experiences into tales of unexpected serendipity or humorous misadventures.

The diversity of items found in these boxes often leads to lively discussions and debates. Some treasure the practical utility of everyday items, while others revel in the novelty of obscure or whimsical objects. These conversations often extend beyond the contents themselves, delving into broader discussions about value, sustainability, and the ethics of consumerism.

For some, the thrill of the mystery box lies in the potential for profit. Reselling valuable items discovered within has become a pursuit in itself, with some individuals honing their skills in identifying hidden gems. These treasure hunters often share tips and tricks, advising newcomers on how to maximize their chances of striking gold. Yet, even among these savvy buyers, the joy of the unknown remains a powerful draw.

The act of sharing these experiences also serves as a form of validation. In the vast sea of consumer choices, the mystery box offers a unique sense of agency and adventure. Each unboxing is a testament to the individual's willingness to embrace uncertainty, to find joy in the unpredictable. It is a reminder that sometimes, the most rewarding experiences are those that defy expectations.

In the end, the community that forms around these shared experiences is perhaps the greatest treasure of all. It is a testament to the power of curiosity and the human desire to connect through storytelling. Whether it is the thrill of discovery, the joy of sharing, or the camaraderie of kindred spirits, the world of Amazon mystery boxes offers a rich tapestry of experiences waiting to be explored.

Learning from Others

As you delve into the world of Amazon mystery boxes, the wisdom of those who have walked this path before can be an invaluable asset. Observing and learning from the experiences of others can provide insights that are not immediately apparent when you first start purchasing these enigmatic collections. By paying attention to the strategies and outcomes of seasoned buyers, you can refine your approach to making these purchases more rewarding and less risky.

One of the first steps in learning from others is to engage with online communities dedicated to Amazon mystery boxes. Platforms such as Reddit, Facebook groups, and specialized forums are treasure troves of information where buyers share their experiences, both good and bad. These communities often have members who are eager to share their knowledge, offering tips on how to identify reputable sellers and avoid potential scams. By actively participating in these discussions, you can glean valuable advice on how to navigate the complexities of purchasing mystery boxes.

Another avenue to consider is watching unboxing videos on platforms like YouTube. Many enthusiasts document their mystery box experiences, providing a visual and narrative account of what they received. These videos can serve as a practical guide, giving you a sense of what to expect in terms of product quality, variety, and the overall value of different types of boxes. Observing the reactions and assessments of these unboxers can help you form realistic expectations and make more informed decisions when selecting a mystery box.

Additionally, reviews on Amazon and other e-commerce sites can be a rich source of information. Buyers often leave detailed feedback about their experiences, including the contents of the boxes they purchased, the condition of the items, and their satisfaction with the overall transaction.

These reviews can highlight patterns, such as which sellers consistently provide high-quality products and which ones might be best avoided. It is important to read a range of reviews, both positive and negative, to gain a balanced understanding of what different mystery boxes have to offer.

Networking with experienced buyers can also be beneficial. Engaging in conversations with individuals who have a track record of successful purchases can provide you with personalized advice and insights. They might share their techniques for researching sellers, the criteria they use to evaluate the potential value of a mystery box, and the strategies they employ to maximize their investment.

Lastly, consider attending events or workshops focused on mystery boxes, if available. These gatherings can offer opportunities to meet other enthusiasts, learn from experts, and even participate in live unboxing sessions. Such events can enhance your understanding of the market dynamics and trends influencing mystery box sales, equipping you with the knowledge needed to make more strategic buying decisions.

By immersing yourself in the experiences and insights of others, you can build a solid foundation of knowledge that will aid you in your journey into the world of Amazon mystery boxes. Observing, questioning, and applying the lessons learned from seasoned buyers can transform your mystery box purchasing from a gamble into a more calculated and enjoyable endeavor.

CHAPTER 12

THE FUTURE OF MYSTERY BOXES

The digital marketplace has undergone a remarkable transformation over the past decade, reshaping the way consumers interact with products and services. The rise of e-commerce has been one of the most significant trends in the retail sector, driven by technological advancements and changing consumer preferences. As more people gain access to the internet and mobile devices, online shopping has become an integral part of daily life, offering convenience, variety, and competitive pricing.

One of the key factors contributing to the growth of ecommerce is the increasing penetration of smartphones and high-speed internet. These technologies have made it easier for consumers to shop online, browse products, and make purchases from the comfort of their homes or on the go. This shift has led to the proliferation of online marketplaces and platforms, with Amazon being a dominant player in the field.

Amazon's influence on e-commerce trends cannot be overstated. The company's customer-centric approach, vast product selection, and efficient delivery systems have set high standards for the industry. As a result, other retailers have been compelled to enhance their online offerings and logistics to remain competitive. The concept of Amazon Mystery Boxes has emerged from this environment, catering to consumers' desire for novelty and surprise in their shopping experiences.

Another trend shaping e-commerce is the increasing emphasis on personalized shopping experiences. With the help of artificial intelligence and big data analytics, online retailers can now offer tailored recommendations and promotions to individual consumers. This personalization enhances customer engagement and satisfaction, leading to higher conversion rates and customer loyalty. As consumers become more accustomed to these customized experiences, the demand for personalized e-commerce solutions continues to grow.

The integration of social media and e-commerce is another significant trend. Platforms like Instagram, Facebook, and TikTok have introduced shopping features that allow users to purchase products directly through the apps. This seamless integration of social media and online shopping not only provides a new channel for retailers to reach potential customers but also leverages the power of social proof and influencer marketing to drive sales.

Sustainability is increasingly becoming a focal point in ecommerce. As consumers become more environmentally conscious, they are seeking out brands and products that align with their values. This has led to a rise in eco-friendly packaging, sustainable sourcing, and ethical business practices among online retailers. Companies that prioritize sustainability are likely to attract a growing segment of conscientious consumers.

The global nature of e-commerce has also opened up opportunities for cross-border shopping. Consumers can now access products from around the world, expanding their choices beyond local retailers. This trend has been facilitated by improvements in international logistics, payment systems, and regulatory frameworks, making it easier for online businesses to tap into new markets.

In this rapidly evolving landscape, businesses must stay attuned to these trends to remain competitive. Understanding the dynamics of e-commerce and adapting to consumer demands are crucial for success in this digital age. As the world of online shopping continues to evolve, the potential for innovation and growth is limitless, offering exciting opportunities for both consumers and businesses alike.

Innovations in Mystery Boxes

The world of Amazon mystery boxes is ever-evolving, driven by the innovative spirit of sellers and the insatiable curiosity of buyers. These boxes, once simple assortments of random items, have transformed into curated experiences that cater to diverse interests and preferences. Sellers have embraced creativity, introducing themes and categories that add a layer of excitement and anticipation to each purchase. From technology gadgets to beauty products, and from rare collectibles to gourmet snacks, the options are as varied as the imaginations of those who assemble them.

113

One of the most striking innovations in mystery boxes is the use of technology to enhance the unboxing experience. Augmented reality (AR) applications are being integrated, allowing buyers to scan their boxes with smartphones and receive interactive hints or clues about the contents. This gamification of the unboxing process adds a new dimension of engagement, transforming a simple opening into an adventure. The integration of digital elements not only heightens the suspense but also offers a personalized touch, as each interaction can be tailored to the buyer's past preferences or purchase history.

Subscription-based mystery boxes have also gained immense popularity, offering consumers the thrill of surprise every month. These subscriptions often come with the promise of exclusive or limited-edition items, creating a sense of urgency and desirability. The subscription model allows sellers to build a loyal customer base, as buyers eagerly anticipate their next delivery, knowing that each box will offer something new and unexpected. This approach has been particularly successful in niches like fashion, where trends change rapidly, and consumers are always on the lookout for the next big thing.

The rise of influencer and celebrity collaborations has further pushed the boundaries of what mystery boxes can offer. Influencers, with their vast reach and niche audiences, bring their unique style and taste into the curation process, resulting in boxes that reflect their personal brand. Fans of these influencers are often drawn to these offerings, eager to own products that have been handpicked by someone they admire. This trend not only boosts sales but also enhances the perceived value of the mystery box, as buyers feel they are getting a piece of the influencer's lifestyle.

Sustainability has also become a key consideration in the evolution of mystery boxes. As consumers become more environmentally conscious, sellers are adopting eco-friendly practices, such as using recyclable packaging and sourcing products from sustainable brands. This not only appeals to the green-minded buyer but also sets a positive precedent for the industry. Some sellers even offer boxes that are entirely focused on sustainability, containing items that promote a zero-waste lifestyle, thus aligning with the values of a growing segment of the market.

In summary, the innovations in Amazon mystery boxes are a testament to the dynamic nature of consumer interests and the adaptability of sellers. By continuously exploring new themes, leveraging technology, and prioritizing sustainability, sellers are able to keep the mystery box concept fresh and exciting, ensuring that the allure of the unknown remains as captivating as ever.

Consumer Preferences

Diving into the world of Amazon mystery boxes, one quickly realizes the diverse array of consumer preferences that shape this unique marketplace. Each buyer approaches these enigmatic parcels with a distinct set of expectations, desires, and motivations. Some are driven by the thrill of the unknown, the tantalizing possibility of unearthing a hidden gem among the assortment of items nestled within the box.

For these adventurous souls, the mystery box represents an opportunity to experience the excitement of a surprise, akin to opening a gift with no prior knowledge of its contents.

On the other hand, there are consumers who are more strategic in their approach, meticulously analyzing past trends, seller reputations, and reviews to make informed purchasing decisions. These individuals often seek out mystery boxes that align with specific interests, such as electronics, fashion, or collectibles, hoping to enhance their collections or discover new products within their preferred categories. For them, the appeal lies not just in the mystery, but also in the potential for value and relevance to their personal tastes.

A significant factor influencing consumer preferences is the perceived value of the contents relative to the price paid. Many buyers are enticed by the prospect of acquiring items worth significantly more than their investment, a gamble that can yield substantial rewards or, conversely, result in disappointment. This element of risk and reward adds an exhilarating dimension to the purchasing process, attracting those who enjoy the challenge of potentially scoring a great deal.

Moreover, the social aspect of buying and unboxing mystery boxes cannot be overlooked. In today's digital age, many consumers are inspired by the trend of sharing their unboxing experiences on social media platforms. This communal activity not only amplifies the excitement and suspense but also fosters a sense of connection and camaraderie among like-minded individuals. Watching others unveil their treasures and reveal their reactions can influence consumer preferences, as potential buyers are swayed by the experiences and recommendations of their peers.

The demographic diversity of consumers also plays a significant role in shaping preferences. Younger buyers, often more tech-savvy and engaged in online communities, may be more inclined towards mystery boxes that feature gadgets or gaming-related items. Meanwhile, older consumers might gravitate towards boxes that promise practical household goods or vintage collectibles. Understanding these demographic nuances is crucial for sellers aiming to tailor their offerings to meet the varied demands of their customer base.

Ultimately, consumer preferences in the realm of Amazon mystery boxes are as varied as the contents of the boxes themselves. They are influenced by a complex interplay of factors, including the allure of surprise, the pursuit of value, social influences, and individual interests. As this market continues to evolve, it is likely that new patterns of preference will emerge, shaped by shifts in consumer behavior and the ever-changing landscape of online commerce. For both buyers and sellers, staying attuned to these preferences is essential to navigating the intriguing and unpredictable world of mystery boxes.

Sustainability and Ethics

Navigating through the world of Amazon mystery boxes, one encounters not just the thrill of surprise and potential value but also the underlying currents of sustainability and ethics. These elements, often overshadowed by the excitement of unboxing, play a pivotal role in shaping consumer practices and industry standards. Understanding the environmental and ethical implications of purchasing and disposing of these boxes is crucial for responsible consumerism.

The sheer volume of goods and packaging involved in the mystery box phenomenon raises significant environmental concerns. Each box, a blend of various items, often includes products that may not be needed or wanted, leading to potential wastage. The packaging itself, frequently excessive to ensure the mystery and protect the contents, contributes to the growing problem of packaging waste. Consumers must consider the environmental footprint of these purchases, including the resources used in production and the impact of disposal.

Moreover, the production and distribution of these boxes often involve complex supply chains that can obscure the ethical practices behind them. Questions arise about the sourcing of the products within these boxes—are they ethically produced? Are they the result of fair labor practices? These concerns are compounded by the anonymity of the items, which can include overstock, returned goods, or even unsold inventory from various sellers. Without transparency, it becomes challenging for consumers to make informed ethical choices.

On the flip side, there is potential for sustainability within the mystery box market. By purchasing mystery boxes, consumers might inadvertently support the circular economy. Items that might otherwise end up as waste find new homes, thus extending their lifecycle and reducing overall waste. This aspect of mystery boxes can be seen as a form of recycling or repurposing, aligning with sustainable practices if approached thoughtfully.

Ethical considerations also extend to the treatment of workers involved in the production and handling of these goods. The supply chain for mystery boxes can include factories and warehouses where labor conditions may not always meet ethical standards. Consumers, increasingly aware of these issues, are beginning to demand greater transparency and accountability from companies offering these products.

For those interested in purchasing Amazon mystery boxes, a balanced approach is essential. It involves being mindful of the environmental impact and the ethical dimensions of these transactions. Researching companies that prioritize sustainable and ethical practices can lead to more responsible purchasing decisions. Furthermore, consumers can take proactive steps by recycling packaging materials and donating unwanted items to reduce waste and promote reuse.

As the popularity of mystery boxes continues to grow, the conversation around sustainability and ethics becomes ever more pertinent. The choices made by consumers today will influence how this market evolves, potentially driving positive changes in production practices and consumer responsibility. By staying informed and considering the broader impact of their purchases, consumers can enjoy the thrill of the mystery box while contributing to a more sustainable and ethical future.

CHAPTER 13

CONCLUSION AND FINAL THOUGHTS

In the intriguing world of Amazon mystery boxes, understanding the fundamental aspects can significantly enhance your purchasing experience. At the core, these mystery boxes are a unique amalgamation of excitement and uncertainty, offering buyers a chance to receive a surprise assortment of items. The allure lies in the unknown, as each box holds a different collection of products that can range from electronic gadgets to household items, and everything in between.

To navigate this fascinating marketplace, it is essential to grasp the key factors that can influence your purchase decision. One of the primary considerations is the reputation of the seller. Since the contents of the boxes are not disclosed, trust becomes a pivotal factor. Researching the seller's history and reading reviews from previous buyers can provide valuable insights into the quality and authenticity of the products within the box.

Another critical element is setting a clear budget. Mystery boxes come in various price ranges, and it's easy to get swept away by the thrill of potentially receiving high-value items at a bargain price. However, it's important to establish how much you are willing to spend and to stick to that limit. This approach not only prevents overspending but also ensures that the experience remains enjoyable rather than stressful.

Understanding the types of mystery boxes available is also beneficial. Some boxes are themed, focusing on specific categories such as electronics, toys, or beauty products, while others are more general. Knowing your preferences can guide you in selecting a box that aligns with your interests, increasing the likelihood of receiving items you will find useful or enjoyable.

Shipping and return policies are additional aspects to consider. Since the contents are unknown, there is always a risk of receiving items that are damaged or not to your liking. Familiarizing yourself with the seller's policies on returns and refunds can provide peace of mind and protect your investment.

Furthermore, the timing of your purchase can play a role in the overall satisfaction of the mystery box experience. Special sales events or holiday seasons might offer enhanced box options or better value for money, as sellers often curate boxes with more appealing items during these times.

Ultimately, the experience of purchasing Amazon mystery boxes is as much about the journey as it is about the destination. The anticipation of unboxing and discovering the contents can be exhilarating, but it is the knowledge and strategies employed beforehand that ensure the process is rewarding. By considering these key points, buyers can approach the world of mystery boxes with confidence, ready to enjoy the surprises that await within each parcel.

As the digital landscape unfurls, a curious phenomenon captures the imagination of adventurous shoppers: the allure of Amazon Mystery Boxes. These enigmatic parcels, each swathed in the promise of surprise and the thrill of the unknown, invite buyers on a unique exploration. The path to acquiring these mysterious bundles is paved with a mixture of anticipation and calculated risk, offering a distinctive experience that is both exhilarating and educational.

Navigating this uncharted territory requires a blend of intuition and strategy. Each box, a tantalizing enigma, holds within its unassuming packaging a world of potential. The contents might range from the mundane to the extraordinary, fostering a sense of discovery that is both personal and shared among a growing community of enthusiasts. The initial allure lies not only in the contents themselves but in the stories they might tell and the connections they might forge.

The process of selecting a mystery box is akin to a treasure hunt, where the clues are hidden in plain sight, waiting to be pieced together by the discerning eye. Online platforms teem with options, each promising a unique assortment of items. Buyers learn to decipher cryptic descriptions, balancing the excitement of the unknown with a pragmatic assessment of value. This delicate dance between expectation and reality becomes an art form in itself, as seasoned shoppers develop a keen sense of discernment.

In this pursuit, patience becomes a trusted companion. The anticipation builds as the box makes its way through the labyrinthine logistics of shipping, each day adding to the crescendo of excitement. Upon arrival, the moment of unveiling is both a personal ritual and a communal celebration. Social media platforms buzz with unboxing videos, where individuals share their discoveries, amplifying the collective joy and occasionally, the shared disappointment.

This shared experience cultivates a sense of camaraderie among enthusiasts. Forums and online communities burgeon with discussions, tips, and tales of the most surprising finds. Through these interactions, buyers not only exchange insights but also forge connections that transcend geographical boundaries. The mystery box experience thus transforms into a vibrant tapestry of human interaction, woven with threads of curiosity and shared passion.

Amidst the thrill of acquisition and the communal exchange of experiences, there lies an opportunity for introspection. Each box, with its medley of surprises, becomes a mirror reflecting personal preferences, desires, and even the occasional impulse. It invites participants to ponder their motivations, to question what drives their fascination with the unknown, and to appreciate the simple joy of discovery.

This exploration into the world of Amazon Mystery Boxes is not merely about the tangible items contained within. It is a journey of self-discovery, a quest for connection, and an invitation to embrace the unpredictability of life. Through each purchase, each unboxing, and each shared story, participants find themselves not only acquiring items but also gaining insights into the nature of curiosity and the timeless allure of mystery.

Final Advice

Navigating the world of Amazon mystery boxes can be an exhilarating experience, filled with the thrill of the unknown and the promise of unexpected treasures. As you venture deeper into this realm, certain strategies and insights can elevate your experience from mere chance to a more informed and satisfying pursuit. Here, we delve into essential tips that can guide you toward making the most out of your mystery box purchases.

Firstly, understanding the seller's reputation is paramount. Not all mystery boxes are created equal, and the integrity of the seller often dictates the quality and authenticity of the items within. Spend time researching the seller's history and customer reviews. Look for consistent positive feedback and any red flags that might indicate a lack of transparency or dissatisfaction among previous buyers. A reputable seller is more likely to offer boxes filled with genuine and valuable items, rather than cheap or counterfeit goods.

Secondly, set a clear budget before diving into the world of mystery boxes. The allure of potential high-value items can be tempting, but it's important to remember that these boxes are, by nature, unpredictable. Allocate an amount that you are comfortable with potentially losing, as there is always a risk involved. By establishing a budget, you can enjoy the experience without financial stress or regret.

Another crucial aspect is understanding the theme or category of the mystery box you are purchasing. Amazon offers a plethora of options, from electronics and fashion to toys and collectibles. Knowing what category piques your interest can significantly enhance your enjoyment and satisfaction. This focus allows you to align your expectations and increases the likelihood of receiving items that you will genuinely appreciate and use.

It's also wise to familiarize yourself with the return and refund policies associated with mystery boxes. While many sellers may offer these boxes as final sales, some do provide limited return options. Understanding these policies beforehand can save you from potential disappointment and ensure you know your rights as a consumer.

Patience is a virtue in the mystery box buying process. Sometimes the most rewarding finds come from waiting for the right box to appear rather than impulsively purchasing the first one that catches your eye. Keep an eye on seasonal promotions or special deals that might offer higher-value items or limited edition boxes. This calculated approach can often yield better results than hasty decisions.

Finally, embrace the experience with an open mind and a sense of adventure. The essence of mystery boxes lies in their unpredictability. While the contents may not always meet your expectations, they offer a unique opportunity to explore new products and brands you might not have considered otherwise. Approach each box with curiosity and excitement, ready to discover what lies within.

In this captivating world of Amazon mystery boxes, armed with these practical tips, you are poised to enhance your journey, making it as enjoyable and rewarding as possible. Whether you're seeking a fun surprise or hoping for a hidden gem, these insights will help you navigate the unknown with confidence and savvy.

Looking Ahead

As enthusiasts and treasure hunters delve deeper into the intriguing world of Amazon mystery boxes, the horizon seems boundless with possibilities. The allure of these enigmatic parcels lies not only in the thrill of uncovering hidden gems but also in the evolving landscape of the ecommerce giant's offerings. With every purchase, there comes an opportunity to discover something unexpected, and as the market grows, so does the variety and potential value of the contents within these boxes.

The current trends suggest a burgeoning interest in niche categories, where buyers seek out mystery boxes tailored to specific interests or hobbies. This shift indicates a future where personalization becomes a key aspect of the mystery box experience. Imagine a box curated specifically for tech enthusiasts, brimming with gadgets and accessories, or one designed for book lovers, filled with rare editions and literary surprises. The potential for customization opens up new avenues for both sellers and buyers, creating a more engaging and satisfying experience.

Moreover, technological advancements are poised to redefine how these boxes are curated and delivered. With the integration of artificial intelligence and machine learning, sellers can better predict consumer preferences and curate boxes that are more likely to delight and surprise. This technological shift not only enhances the buying experience but also ensures that the contents are more aligned with the buyer's interests, thereby increasing the perceived value of each purchase.

The community aspect of buying and sharing experiences related to Amazon mystery boxes is also expected to grow. Online platforms and social media channels provide spaces for enthusiasts to connect, share unboxing experiences, and exchange tips on where to find the best deals. As this community expands, it fosters a sense of camaraderie and shared excitement, making the experience of buying mystery boxes not just a solitary endeavor but a social one.

In addition, sustainability is becoming a significant consideration in the future of mystery boxes. As consumers become more environmentally conscious, there is a growing demand for eco-friendly packaging and responsibly sourced products. Sellers who prioritize sustainability in their offerings are likely to attract a more conscientious customer base, thus setting a new standard in the industry.

The regulatory landscape may also evolve, with potential guidelines to ensure transparency and fairness in the sale of mystery boxes. Buyers may look forward to more detailed descriptions and assurances regarding the quality and condition of the items within, which could enhance trust and encourage more people to try their luck with these intriguing packages.

In this ever-changing environment, the excitement of purchasing Amazon mystery boxes is bound to endure, driven by innovation, community engagement, and a commitment to sustainability. As the market adapts to new consumer demands and technological advancements, the mystery box phenomenon is set to remain a captivating and dynamic facet of online shopping. Whether you're a seasoned collector or a curious newcomer, the future holds endless possibilities for discovery and delight.

Made in United States
Orlando, FL
30 November 2024

54689723R00075